D1389530

THE
LITTLE
BOOK
OF
SURREY

RUPERT MATTHEWS

First published 2010

The History Press
The Mill, Brimscombe Port
Stroud, Gloucestershire, GL5 2QG
www.thehistorypress.co.uk

British Library Cataloguing in Publication Data.
A catalogue record for this book is available from the British Library.

ISBN 978 0 7524 5633 1
Typesetting and origination by The History Press
Printed in Great Britain

CONTENTS

INTRODUCTION

Surrey is one of the most charming of English counties, but for those who think they know it, there are some surprises in store. The county is not all suburban gardens, rolling hills and quiet villages. History has been made here, tragedy has struck and fortune has smiled.

Surrey folk today might not notice, but the bridge they drive over may be 700 years old, or might be only the latest in a string of bridges that go back to Roman times. They may, if they go shopping in Epsom, make a purchase in a shop that was once home to Nell Gwyn, the witty mistress of Charles II. Others unknowingly walk on battlefields where brave men fought and died for the causes they believed in.

Those who think Surrey is a peaceful place might be surprised to hear that the army had to be called out to end a riot in Guildford that left houses in flames and a policeman dead. And there have been brutal murders aplenty; some of the killers ended up swinging from a gibbet, but others got away with their brutal crimes.

Not everything in Surrey has been a success either. Take the grandly named Staines, Wokingham & Woking Junction Railway which never got as far as Woking. Then there was the great playwright Richard Brinsley Sheridan who moved to Leatherhead to find peace and quiet in which to work, but who got so distracted by the fine fishing that he didn't write a single word the whole time he was there.

But Surrey is not all about the past. There is plenty to be seen today, be it theatres or country walks, wildlife or fine churches. Wherever you are going in Surrey, slip this book into your pocket and prepare to be surprised.

1

CRIME & PUNISHMENT

HIGHWAYMEN

The Golden Farmer

Bagshot Heath was once reputedly the most dangerous place in England – all because of the activities of a particularly cool, violent and careful highwayman who operated there from about 1647 to 1689. This particular highwayman was known for the guile that he used. He once rode up to a gentleman and told him that there were two disreputable men hanging about the heath and suggested that they travel together for safety. The

A highwayman confronts the gibbet that stood on Bagshot Heath. This area of virtually uninhabited country was a notorious haunt of robbers and criminals of all kinds.

gentleman agreed, adding that he had 50 guineas on him but that they were sewn into a secret panel of his coat and so would be safe from robbers. After riding for a while, the highwayman remarked conversationally, 'I believe here is nobody will take the pains of robbing you or me today. Therefore I think I had as good take the trouble upon me of robbing you myself, so pray give me your coat.' He produced a pistol and a sword to enforce his demands.

Another victim came in for rougher treatment. Four ladies in a coach were stopped on Bagshot Heath by the highwayman. Three of them handed over their jewellery but the fourth, an elderly Quaker, said she had nothing of value on her. The highwayman punched her to the ground and shouted, 'You canting bitch, are you so greedy as to lose your life for the sake of Mammon. Come, come, open your purse quickly or else I shall send you out of the land of the living.' His sword then found the lady's neck and prodded, at which point she produced a purse of gold coins and a diamond ring.

One of the puzzles about this particular highwayman was that nobody who was robbed either recognised him or saw him again. It was almost as if he robbed, then vanished. The man's luck ran out in November 1689 when a former victim

A highwayman of the early eighteenth century. The years 1690 to 1730 were the heyday of highwaymen as the authorities had not yet instituted an effective force to police the open roads.

recognised him drinking in a tavern in Fleet Street, London, and called the watch. The notorious highwayman of Bagshot Heath turned out to be an apparently law-abiding farmer in Gloucestershire named William Davis. This Davis lived a blameless life on his farm, but went on frequent visits to London returning with large amounts of money that he said he had won at the gaming tables. So much wealth did Davis bring home that his neighbours nicknamed him the 'Golden Farmer'. He was hanged before the year was out.

The Roaring Girl

One of the few highwaywomen on record also robbed on the heaths of north Surrey. Mary Frith (more famously known as Moll Cutpurse) spent most of her criminal career as a fence, receiving and selling-on stolen goods, but in the conditions of chaos of the English Civil War she decided to try her hand at highway robbery. In 1651 she and her henchmen stopped a coach that was carrying no less a person than Sir Thomas Fairfax, commander-in-chief of the Parliamentary armed forces.

The frontispiece for a version of the popular play The Roaring Girle, *which was based on the colourful criminal career of Surrey girl Mary Frith.*

She got away with a hefty £250, but Fairfax was furious and had the authority to organise a massive operation against highwaymen near London. Frith was caught, but bought her freedom by paying a fine of £2,000 – then a colossal sum of cash. She then wisely turned honest to evade the notice of the authorities. She died in 1659 and left £20 in her will to fund a party for named individuals should England ever become a kingdom again, which it did the following year. A play about her life, called *The Roaring Girle*, was written with her assistance.

The Butcher of Bagshot

James Whitney was a butcher's son from Hertfordshire who tired of the hard work involved in his father's trade at a young age. He then ran off to London to lead a life of petty crime, heavy drinking and wanton womanising.

In 1683, at the age of twenty-three, Whitney decided that he needed to improve himself. He bought himself an elegant suit of fine clothes together with a rapier and a pistol, then stole the best horse he could lay his hands on and became a highwayman. Because many of the first highwaymen had been gentlemen fallen on hard times through supporting the king in the Civil War, the criminal classes looked up to highwaymen as being a social cut above mere pickpockets and burglars. Whitney ostentatiously lived up to the ideal by wearing flashy jewellery, exquisitely tailored suits and behaving with impeccable politeness at all times – even when holding a gun to a man's head he remembered to say please and thank you.

By 1690 Whitney was leading a gang of some fifty men. Not all of them rode with him, some lolled about in inns looking for rich victims, others fenced stolen goods and at least one worked for the Surrey magistrates to keep an eye on what they were doing. It was this spy who reported that Mr William Hull had sworn that he would one day watch Whitney ride his horse backwards – a reference to the fact that men to be hanged were

A contemporary engraving of James Whitney in prison awaiting execution. the inset shows his famous encounter with William Hull.

taken to the gallows tied sitting backwards on a horse. Whitney led his gang to waylay Hull a week later. The unfortunate man was robbed, then tied backwards on his saddle and let loose across Bagshot Heath while the highwaymen jeered at him.

Whitney was getting bolder. One of his spies reported that a gentleman in a coach was carrying a chest filled with gold and silver coins and was escorted by a dozen dragoons. Whitney rounded up forty of his gang and launched an attack on the dragoons and the coach. But his spy had got things wrong: the twelve dragoons were only the advance of a guard totalling over fifty men. The gentleman in the coach was the Duke of Marlborough, hero of the wars against the French and he was not about to hand over his army's pay chest to a common highwayman. A pitched battle ensued that saw ten of

Whitney's men killed and others captured and wounded. One of those wounded men talked to save his own life and Whitney was soon arrested. He was hanged in December 1692. Mr Hull was watching.

Jack Rann

Perhaps the best dressed highwayman active in Surrey was Jack Rann, nicknamed 'Sixteen String Jack' because he wore sixteen ribbons about his knees – then a great fashion among gentlemen. Officially Rann was a self-employed coachman who hired himself and his coach out to whomever had need of it, but few people ever saw him work. The act was merely a cover for his criminal activities. Like Whitney before him, Rann ostentatiously adopted fine clothes and fine manners, especially when at work on the roads. In 1773 he appeared at

A contemporary engraving of Jack Rann at his trial. Rann was a notorious criminal, but was at least as well known for his outstanding fashion sense.

the Barnet Races in a blue silk three-piece suit trimmed with lace woven from pure silver thread, and he created quite a sensation. When he was finally arrested in September 1774 he called for a tailor to make him a new suit of pea green wool trimmed with silver lace, and he bought a selection of ruffled linen shirts so that he could have a fresh shirt for each day of his trial. After being found guilty he threw a series of parties in prison, the last of which was for seven of his girlfriends. He was hanged the next day, in yet another new suit.

UNSOLVED MURDERS

The Wrecclesham Groom

On 17 April 1904 the body of sixteen-year-old horsegroom George White was found in Forest Row, Wrecclesham. He had been hit over the head with a heavy stick, after which his throat had been cut. Police discovered that shortly before, White had started courting a girl named Mary who had previously been seeing an eighteen-year-old named Frank Fry. Fry was arrested, questioned and charged with murder. However, the police were unable to find any evidence firmly linking him to the murder so, despite a fair amount of circumstantial evidence, he was set free. The crime was never solved.

The Hogg Sisters

At 5 p.m. on 11 June 1906 the postman called at the home of the elderly Hogg sisters in Heathfield. The door was open but nobody answered his call, so he looked inside to find Mary Hogg, sixty-eight, lying dead on the floor. The other sister, Caroline, aged sixty-two, was lying beside her, alive, but drenched in blood. Police and a doctor were called. Both women had been struck on the head with a hammer and then stabbed with a knife but neither weapon was to be found. When she recovered her senses, Caroline said that a scruffy-looking man had knocked on the door claiming to be unemployed and asking for food. Mary had not liked him and had refused, whereupon the man burst in and attacked the two women. Nobody was ever arrested for the murder and assault.

The Cutt Mill Killings

On the evening of 8 October 1932 an odd-job man called at Cutt Mill to discuss some work with the owners, Mr and Mrs Keen. He found Mrs Keen lying dead on the kitchen floor with her throat cut and a meal cooking on the stove. He ran off to fetch the police. The police quickly found Mr Keen floating dead in a nearby pond and that a large sum of money that the Keens had owned was missing. Almost as quickly the police found a gamekeeper in nearby woods who told them that he had seen a man acting suspiciously in the woods near Cutt Mill that afternoon, and said the man was a local called Godfrey Nobes. The police promptly arrested Nobes, who was found to own a jacket with bloodstains on it. At his trial, Nobes claimed the blood came from a nosebleed. There was no other evidence against him and he was found not guilty. Nobes immediately booked himself a ticket to Australia and was never heard from again. In 2002, Nobes' jacket was subjected to new tests that showed the blood was not his and that it had sprayed from in front, not fallen from above. Nobes had been guilty, but he had got away with it and the case remains officially unsolved.

SENSATIONAL MURDERS

The Unknown Sailor

On 22 September 1786 a sailor stopped at the Bear Hotel in Esher. He told the landlord that he was walking to Portsmouth from London to look for work on a ship. The sailor was clearly better set up than most, for he paid his overnight bill with a golden guinea and pocketed the silver change. The same sailor stopped again at the Red Lion near Thursley. He left next morning in the company of three other men who had stayed the night at the inn. Later that day two cottagers spotted a dead body, stripped naked and lying in the Devil's Punch Bowl a couple of miles south of Thursley. They carried the body to the Red Lion where the landlord recognised it as that of the wealthy sailor. Men were sent riding in all directions, and one found the three men in Petersfield in the process of selling the dead man's clothes. They were arrested, tried and hanged beside the Portsmouth Road where it curves around the Devil's Punch Bowl. The gibbet was still there in the 1820s, but has now been replaced by an upright stone which bears the inscription:

> Erected in detestation of a barbarous murder committed here on an unknown sailor on Sepr. 24th 1786 by Edwd Lonegan, Michale Casey and Jas Marshall, who were all taken the same day and hung in chains on this place.

THE CHALKPIT MURDER

On 30 November 1946 a dead body was found dumped in a chalkpit at Woldingham. The body was soon identified as that of John Mudie, a barman from Wimbledon. Police rapidly found that Mudie had been seeing a woman named Maggie Brook and concluded that Brook's long-term lover, Thomas Ley, was the prime suspect. That was when they hit a problem: Thomas Ley was not only a very rich and well-respected businessman, he was also a former MP and minister in the Australian Government. Treading carefully, the Surrey police contacted the Australian police. They found that – although nothing had been proved – Ley was suspected of at least two murders in Australia and that some of his business dealings had been highly dubious. The break came when a man working for Ley told police that he had been paid by Ley to follow Mudie for some days before the murder – Ley's story had been that the Mudie was a blackmailer. Ley was found guilty of the murder, but was judged to be insane and was sent to Broadmoor where he remained until his death.

THE PRINCE OF WALES' NURSE

On 11 June 1854 a man walking down Church Street, Esher, noticed a dark liquid oozing out from under a front door. He bent down and was horrified to find it was blood. The man kicked the door open to find a woman lying on the floor with her throat cut and a razor lying beside her. He staunched the blood with a handkerchief while shouting out to passers-by to fetch a doctor and a policeman. Both arrived promptly and while the doctor tended the woman, PC Martell investigated the rest of the house. He found six children, all dead, who had had their throats cut. The woman was found to be the householder, Mrs Mary Brough, a local wet nurse who had tended the Prince of Wales during Queen Victoria's visits to nearby Claremont. Her husband, George Brough, had left her two days earlier telling friends that he suspected Mary of having an affair. He vowed that he would take the children away from her as soon as he had found a house to rent. When Mary Brough recovered consciousness it was quite clear that she was insane. She calmly confessed to the murders of her six children and was later sent to an asylum.

THE CHURCHYARD MURDER

On Sunday 4 August 1901 Mr and Mrs Alfred Heaver of Westcott were walking to the morning church service, along with most of the other villagers. They had just reached the gate to the churchyard when a young man stepped up to them and said, 'Hello, Alfred.' The man then pulled out a revolver and shot Mr Heaver in the chest. Mr Heaver collapsed, whereupon the man bent forward, put the gun to the wounded man's head and fired twice more. The man then calmly walked off towards Dorking railway station. Having recovered from their shock and horror, four of the villagers gave chase. When the man saw them, he turned the gun on himself and blew his brains out. It transpired that the gunman was Mrs Heaver's brother, who had an imagined grievance against his brother-in-law.

THE PHOTOGRAPHED MURDERER

At 3.20 p.m. on 27 June 1881, the ticket inspector meeting the express from London found a young man covered in blood and missing his shirt collar groggily staggering from a first-class compartment on to the platform. The man gave his name as Percy Lefroy and said that he had been attacked by two large, burly men as the train ran through Merstham Tunnel. He said he had fought back, thought he had hit one of the men badly but had then passed out and recovered his senses only as the train arrived in Brighton. A Brighton policeman, John Holmes, offered to escort the man home to the address in Wallington that he had given. Having done so, Holmes reported to the local police station to find that the man calling himself Lefroy was now wanted for murder. The body of a wealthy businessman named Isaac Gold had been found by the trackside south of Merstham together with Lefroy's shirt collar. A large sum of money and a valuable gold watch with which Gold had left home were missing. Holmes raced back to Lefroy's house but the culprit had gone. He had, however, left behind papers showing that his real name was Percy Lefroy Mapleton as well as a photograph of himself. A line sketch based on the photograph was printed in the press, leading to the prompt arrest of Mapleton, who was hanged on 29 November that year.

THE HALF-CROWN KILLER

In 1888 a man claiming to be an artist living on a private income of £500 per year, and earning additional money from the sale of his paintings, came to live in Godalming using the name Samuel Wheatcroft. He was, in fact, a conman named Ebenezer Jenkins who had spun a similar tale elsewhere only to abscond without paying rent and without repaying cash he had borrowed from gullible locals. In Godalming he struck up a romance with eighteen-year-old Emily Joy. He proposed marriage and, to calm the suspicions of the girl's father, wrote down an entirely fictitious account of his supposed income and a large inheritance he claimed to be expecting. On 10 January, Emily went to visit 'Wheatcroft' at his studio. There Wheatcroft apparently tried to seduce her, but she refused and a fight began in the course of which the girl was strangled. Wheatcroft fled to the nearby Sun Inn where he ordered several drinks and meal. He tried to pay the bill with a half-crown that Emily wore as a brooch. The landlord recognised the brooch, thought it suspicious that Emily would part with it, and sent a boy running to investigate. The killing was soon uncovered and a policeman came to arrest Wheatcroft, who was found guilty of murder and hanged. 'I have never known a more revolting murder,' said the judge as he passed sentence.

READING THE RIOT ACT AT GODALMING

In 1715 a new law came into force. It was called 'An Act for preventing Tumults and Riotous Assemblies, and for the more speedy and effectual Punishing the Rioters', but was soon much better known as the Riot Act. Taking part in a riot had long been a criminal offence, with death being the penalty if loss of life occurred during the disturbance. What the Riot Act did was to give magistrates the power to declare that a riot was taking place as it was doing so, and gave them the power to forcibly break up a rioting mob using any means that came to hand. If people were killed by the magistrates or the men – usually soldiers – they used, then it was held that they had been lawfully killed. In practice a magistrate had to read out the following statement from the Riot Act:

Our Sovereign Lord the King chargeth and commandeth
that all persons being assembled immediately to disperse
and peaceably to depart to their habitations, or to their
lawful business, upon the pains contained in the act made in
the first year of King George the First for preventing tumults
and riotous assembles. God save the King.

After that, lethal force could be used to break up the event. Understandably, reading out the Riot Act was considered a very serious step that was not to be taken lightly. Conversely, the mere sight of a magistrate with a piece of paper in his hands and soldiers on hand was often enough to stop a riot instantly – nobody wanted to be the first to be shot.

The last time that the Riot Act was read in Surrey was on 5 November 1929 at Chiddingfold. That village had (and still has) a proud tradition of huge celebrations on Bonfire Night, but in 1928 there had been some drunken violence. The local policeman, Sergeant Charles Brake, was determined that there would be no repeat and spent the second half of October 1929 cracking down on the local young men and warning all and sundry that he would not tolerate any nonsense come the big day. On 2 November somebody lit the village bonfire. The villagers blamed Brake, and hostility against him grew. The village constable, Eric Roster, informed his superiors that he was worried about how events might turn out. As a result, six big, burly policemen were sent to Chiddingfold on the afternoon of 5 November along with County Magistrate Mr Short, who had the Riot Act in his pocket. Two charabanc-loads of policemen were gathered in Guildford police station ready to be despatched if the need arose.

Just after dark fell, Brake and Roster went to the village green to patrol the festival. The bonfire was lit and the crowd turned ugly. Fireworks were thrown at the two policemen, so the six constables marched out to support them. More fireworks were thrown, along with bottles and rocks. The policemen retreated to the police house, where Mr Short was waiting for them. The house came under siege with bricks, fireworks and stones being thrown to smash the windows. There was a real danger that the place might be set on fire, so Mr Short phoned Guildford and the two bus-loads of reinforcements set out. Short, meanwhile, went out to talk to the mob. He gathered that they wanted Brake moved from the village, and announced that this would happen but only if the crowd all went home. Nobody moved. At this point the police reinforcements arrived. Short climbed up on to a wall and pulled the Riot Act from his pocket. The police charged, flailing about them with their truncheons and scattered the crowd. Within five minutes it was all over, the green had been cleared and the policemen patrolled the village, arresting anyone they found out of doors. Contrary to popular belief, however, Short always maintained that he had never actually read the Riot Act.

THE WITLEY RIOT

In 1919 several hundred Canadian soldiers based at Witley Camp south of Godalming got fed up waiting to be sent home now that the First World War was over. There were sporadic outbursts of drunkenness and ill-discipline before, one night, a full-scale riot broke out. Hundreds of soldiers demonstrated against poor rations, not being sent home and also what they saw as heavy-handed punishments meted out to their fellows. They attacked the local military prison and released all the Canadians being held. They then moved on to Witley where they broke into shops and pubs to get hold of drink – and set fire to a tailor's shop. The aggrieved tailor took legal action against the Surrey police claiming that the events that night met every legal definition of a riot and that the police should have had the Riot Act read out and dispersed the rioting soldiers. The case came to court in front of Lord Sterndale on 2 January 1923. The court found that the tailor was right, the police were wrong, and that the police therefore had to pay for the burned shop and all the stock lost by the tailor.

THE OXTED RIOT

In 1866 the Surrey & Sussex Junction Railway began work on a line running from Croydon to Tunbridge Wells via Oxted. The construction was not all it seemed, however. The company was in reality a front for the much larger London, Brighton & South Coast Railway (LB&SCR) which was not supposed to build into Kent, then the preserve of the South Eastern Railway (SER). Waring Construction was hired as the main building company and work began.

Easily the most complex part of the proposed line was a tunnel running for 506 yards through Tandridge Hill, just north of Oxted. Such works were expensive, but money was tight so Warings took a dramatic step. They sent an agent to Belgium to hire large numbers of unemployed factory workers to come to Surrey to provide the bulk of the unskilled labour. This did not go down well with the established British railway construction workers, or 'navvies'.

In an effort to keep the two gangs of tough workmen apart, Warings sent the British workers to construct the southern section of the line. A large camp of temporary wooden accommodation was built for the British works at Blackham in Sussex, while the camp for the Belgians was pitched just outside Oxted.

All went well until September when two Belgian workers bumped into a group of English navvies in a pub. A scuffle broke out, which ended with the Belgians running off. They came back with many more of their colleagues and a large-scale fight broke out. The police were called and the two groups of navvies were separated and escorted back to their respective camps. PC Nathan Tobutt was posted on the road through Edenbridge that linked the two camps. Exactly what happened next is unclear, but it involved a young woman by the name of Rosalie Martin who was on very friendly terms with a Belgian. Tobutt spotted a large group of English navvies heading north through the fields toward Oxted. He sprinted off to alert his superiors.

By the time the police arrived at the Oxted camp the place was in uproar. Young Miss Martin was being held by two English navvies and was heavily bruised. Fights were taking place across a wide area of Surrey countryside and large numbers of hapless Belgians were hiding in the snow-covered woods clad in nothing but their nightshirts. The police waded in to make mass arrests and drive the two groups of men apart.

At the subsequent trial, two of the English navvies were each sent to prison for two months. Of the Belgians there was no sign; they had skipped bail and fled back to their homeland. Work on the railway line ceased soon afterwards, though the route was later finished off as a joint project by the SER and LB&SCR.

THE GUILDFORD RIOTS

What have become known as the Guildford Riots were not, in origin, anything of the kind. In the days before social workers and a regular police force were ever dreamed of, local communities had a way of sorting out local problems. If a person was known to be guilty of anti-social, but not illegal, behaviour he or she would be subjected to what was loosely known as Rough Music. Wife-beaters, malicious gossips, bad payers, seducers of servants and others would find their house surrounded by a crowd banging pots and pans, blowing whistles and shouting insults. If an offender did not take the hint and change his behaviour, events could escalate. The Rough Music would be repeated, but this time a group of muscular young men would be sent in to drag the malefactor outside to be thrown in a pond, tied to a pole, paraded around the village or to have something of value or use taken from them. Food or drink was often taken and shared out among the crowd.

In Guildford the usual punishment was for a piece of furniture to be removed from the house, taken to the top of the High Street and burned. The traditional day on which Guildford folk indulged in Rough Music was on 5 November. A mob would parade through the town, stopping outside the houses of those deemed guilty of some misdemeanour. A piece of furniture, section of fence or some other wooden objects would be removed and carried to the High Street. By the end of the day a sizeable pile would have been collected, which was then set on fire as part of the Guy Fawkes Night celebrations.

In 1843 the then new Surrey Constabulary decided that such old-fashioned notions of dealing with wrong-doers had to stop.

They arrested the two men who had organised that year's Guy Fawkes Night and charged them with affray. The magistrates were as keen as the police to stamp out such proceedings and imposed heavy fines. The plan misfired when a collection among the townsfolk met the bill.

Thereafter the Guys wore masks, but this and the publicity began to cause a change in the event. Men from outside the town began arriving to take part, enjoying the opportunities for violence and destruction. By 1854 things were getting out of hand, but many locals were unwilling to give up their traditional right to impose punishment on wrong-doers. There was a strong feeling that the attempt to ban the Guy Fawkes events were led by local employers who had been targetted for paying low wages and unfairly dismissing workers. By 1861, however, things were more serious as several buildings went up in flames.

The turning point seems to have been 1864 when a policeman was killed. The locals were still divided over whether to continue with the event or not, but all agreed that the outside toughs were causing the worst of the violence and had to be stopped. A new mayor dedicated to stopping what by now were termed 'riots' was elected in the shape of Mr P. Jacob. On the morning of 5 November 1865 a long column of 300 policemen marched into Guildford, accompanied by a squadron of 50 cavalrymen and 140 infantrymen. The cavalry took up station outside the church at the top of the High Street, their razor-sharp lances glistening in the autumn sunshine. The soldiers waited at the railway station and on the main roads leading into Guildford. Anyone they did not like the look of was turned away. Police patrolled the streets and broke up any groups of men who looked likely to cause any trouble. For the next four years, Mayor Jacob repeated the precautions, but in 1870 nobody showed any sign of turning out for the traditional event and in 1871 no soldiers or extra police were brought in. There was no trouble. The riots were over.

2

ROYAL SURREY

ROYAL LOVERS

In 1667 Lord Buckhurst rented no. 36 High Street, Epsom, for the summer and moved in with his mistress Nell Gwyn. At the time she was the most admired, most highly paid and most popular comedy actress on the London stage. Buckhurst did not keep her for long. King Charles II was a frequent visitor to Epsom to take the salts – and he noticed the pretty young red-headed actress. On 11 October Buckhurst got involved in a drunken brawl that ended with his being thrown naked into the local gaol. Gwyn packed her bags and left to take up the offer already made to her by the king. She was to remain his mistress to the end of his life. Indeed, his dying words were 'Let not poor Nelly starve.'

ROYAL DEATHS

1036, Alfred the Atheling

For the year 1036 the *Anglo-Saxon Chronicle* records an incident that took place just outside Guildford. The two men involved were Alfred the Atheling, eldest son of the former king, Ethelred the Unready, and Godwin, Earl of Wessex. At the time King Canute, who had ousted Ethelred, had only just died and his two sons were squabbling over the inheritance. Harold Harefoot was favoured in England as his mother had been English, while Harthacanute was more popular in Denmark as he was fully Danish. It was at this point that Alfred decided to visit England. He said he was coming to see his mother, who was living in retirement at Winchester, but it seems fair to assume he wanted to gauge support for himself. Earl Godwin, meanwhile, was the leading nobleman in England. His father had been a fairly minor nobleman in Sussex, but he had risen to greatness by a combination of skill and a judicious marriage to a cousin of Canute named Gytha. At this date Godwin had not yet declared whom he supported to be King of England, though it was rumoured that he favoured Harold Harefoot.

According to the *Chronicle*, written within a few weeks of the event, 'As Alfred and his men approached the town of Guildford in Surrey, thirty miles south-west of London, they were met by the powerful Earl Godwin of Wessex, who professed loyalty to the young prince and procured lodgings for him and his men in the town. The next morning, Godwin said to Alfred, "I will safely and securely conduct you to London, where the great men of the kingdom are awaiting your coming, that they may raise you to the throne." Then the earl led the prince and his men over the hill of Guildown, which is to the west of Guildford, on the road to Winchester, not London. Perhaps the prince had insisted on continuing his journey to his original destination, his mother's court in Winchester, in any case, Godwin repeated his tempting offer; showing the prince the magnificent panorama from the hill both to the north and to the south, he said, "Look around on the right hand and on the left, and behold what a realm will be subject to your dominion." Alfred then gave thanks to God and promised that if he should ever be crowned king, he would institute such laws as would be pleasing and acceptable to God and men. At that moment, however, he was seized and bound together with all his men. Nine tenths of them were then murdered. And since the remaining tenth was still so numerous, they, too, were decimated. Alfred was tied to a horse and his eyes were put out. Soon after this he died.' Some versions have him dying in captivity on the Isle of Ely, but die he most certainly did.

1817, Princess Charlotte Augusta

Princess Charlotte Augusta of Wales was born in London on 7 January 1796 as the only child of Prince George of Wales, later to be King George IV. She was, therefore, the heir to the throne of Great Britain and Ireland. In 1816 she married Prince Leopold of Saxe-Coburg-Saalfeld, a minor German princeling who was considered intelligent and steady but not so important as to be a threat to Charlotte when she inherited the throne. The young couple moved to Claremont House, just outside Esher. In 1817 Princess Charlotte fell pregnant. After a difficult pregnancy she went into labour on 3 November. She was delivered of a still-born son, and died herself three days later. The doctor, Sir Richard Croft, blamed his failure to use forceps for the tragedy and shot himself. An elegant and moving memorial to Princess Charlotte can be found in St George's Church, Esher. Her widower went on to be chosen as king of the newly created Belgium in 1830 for the same reasons that he was chosen to be husband to Princess Charlotte.

1513, James IV of Scotland

This Scottish king invaded England in 1513 at the head of one of the largest armies ever fielded by the Scots. This did not save him from being both defeated and killed on Flodden Field, in Northumberland, on 9 September. His body was embalmed and taken to London where it was paraded through the streets. King Henry VIII then sent the body to Sheen Abbey, in Surrey, but would pay for neither a funeral nor a tomb. The body remained in a storeroom until the abbey was closed down in the Reformation. Nobody knows what became of the royal body.

ROYAL RESIDENCES

Nonsuch Palace

In 1537 a long-awaited son and heir was born to King Henry VIII. The delighted king decided that only a grand new house would be suitable for his son. The house had to be luxurious, close to London and untainted by any connections to previous royal failures.

Henry's eye fell on the village of Cuddington which he owned and which lay adjacent to Stane Street, the main London–Chichester road. Henry ordered the entire village to be removed to make way for a grand new house. Construction work began in April 1538 and was completed three years later. As royal palaces went, Cuddington was not particularly large but it was sumptuous to an unprecedented degree. Indeed, it soon acquired the nickname of Nonsuch since there was none such palace like it.

Nonsuch Palace as it looked in the reign of Queen Elizabeth I. No trace of this bizarre building now remains above ground.

The palace remained in royal hands until 1670, though it does not seem to have been used very much after the reign of Queen Elizabeth I. Certainly when Charles II gave it to his mistress Countess Barbara of Castlemaine, she complained about the state of the place. Indeed after some half-hearted attempts at renovation, she had the entire building pulled down and sold the materials. The wooden panelling from Nonsuch now lines the rooms at Loseley House, Guildford, and other architectural features survive in other properties around the south of England. Nothing was left above ground, with only some of the foundations left in situ to be found by an archaeological dig in 1959.

In 1731 a new Nonsuch mansion was built on the estate, but it has never had any royal connections. Owing to boundary changes, Nonsuch is now in Greater London.

Oatlands Palace

In 1540 King Henry VIII annulled his marriage to Anne of Cleves, whom Henry found so repulsive that he was unable to consummate the marriage. Anne's family did not want her back, so Henry was left with the problem of what to do with her. He hit on the idea of making her his 'sister' and endowing her with estates befitting a royal princess. Among these was Oatlands Manor, just outside Weybridge. Oatlands was conveniently located close enough to London that Anne could attend court whenever invited, but not so close that she would be an embarrassment to the king's love life. Just as convenient were the huge empty buildings of Chertsey Abbey, closed down by Henry in 1537. Great quantities of stones, bricks and glass were taken from the redundant abbey to build a new house fit for Anne. The grand house was built around three interlinked courtyards. Together with the stables, servants' quarters, privy garden and outhouses, Oatlands grew to cover 28 acres.

A view of the vanished Oatlands Palace as it was in the early 1600s.

After Anne of Cleves died in 1557, Oatlands reverted to the crown. It was used as a handy bolthole away from London by first Queen Mary I, and then by Queen Elizabeth I. After Elizabeth's death the house was taken over by Anne, queen to James I. She valued the house as a private escape from the business of court and went there to relax whenever she could. Inigo Jones was employed to add some embellishments to the façade to make the house look more fashionable. The house then passed to Henrietta Maria, queen to Charles I, who used it for a similar purpose as had her mother-in-law. After Charles I was executed, the palace was confiscated by Parliament, which then sold it to a speculator who had nearly all of it demolished and sold the materials to local builders. Only one small wing was left standing.

That remainder and the estate passed through various hands until the 1770s when it was bought by Henry Clinton, Duke of Newcastle. He enlarged the house and laid out new gardens. He then sold it to the Duke of York, third son of King George III, so that Oatlands once again became a royal residence. The Yorks used the house not so much to escape London as to invite London to the country. They invited all the most fashionable leaders of society to Oatlands, including the composer Haydn and man of fashion Beau Brummell. After the death of the Duchess of York in 1820 the house was sold to Edward Hughes Ball who had it rebuilt into Italianate style, as it remains to this day. In 1856 the house became a hotel, as it is today.

Claremont House

The Claremont Estate was created in 1714 for the Earl of Clare, who named it Clare Mount. In 1768 the estate was bought by Robert Clive, a general who had made a vast fortune in India. He pulled down Clare's modest home and spent a vast fortune having the grounds remodelled by Capability Brown and a new house constructed in the fashionable Palladian style. It is Clive's house that survives. In 1816 the estate was bought by the nation as a wedding present for Princess Charlotte, who died in childbirth in 1817. Her widower, Prince Leopold, used the house as his British residence thereafter. Among the many guests who stayed here regularly was young Princess Victoria who in 1837 became Queen Victoria and promptly bought the estate for herself. Victoria used Claremont as a country retreat from which she could return quickly to London if she needed to.

Victoria did not use the house for long, however. In 1848 a revolution broke out in France and King Louis-Philippe hurried into exile rather than risk execution. Victoria gave him Claremont as a home for him and his wife, Queen Anna. Louis-Philippe died in 1850, but Anna survived until 1866. The house was then given by Victoria to her fourth son, Leopold, who was created Duke of Albany. In 1900 his son Charles inherited the small German duchy of Saxe-Coburg-Gotha which had belonged to Victoria's husband Prince Albert. Charles then moved to Germany to take up his throne, but his widowed mother remained in residence at Claremont. In 1914, war broke out between Britain and Germany. After some hesitation, Charles joined the German Army as an officer, though he never held any high commands. In 1917 a legal ruling in another case meant that by fighting on the German side while still holding his British title of Duke of Albany, Charles was guilty of treason for which the mandatory penalty was death. After Germany surrendered, Charles gave up his Albany title and the British government deprived him of Claremont. The grand house passed through a number of private hands until in 1930 it was bought by a public school, which is still in residence.

Guildford Castle

This fine castle was begun on the orders of William the Conqueror in 1066. At the time he had defeated and killed King Harold Godwinson on the bloody field of Hastings on 14 October, but had not yet secured the throne of England – there were other claimants around including Edgar the Atheling who, as grandson of King Edmund II, had a better claim than did William. London had shut its gates against William, who decided to march around the city, building castles to block reinforcements marching to the city. The castle at Guildford guarded both the main east–west route along the downs and the important north–south River Wey. At first it was a simple earthen mound topped by a wooden tower – a motte – but it was soon expanded to be a more complex structure. In 1170 the huge stone keep was added, with stone walls and other towers coming later. Throughout its history, Guildford was a royal castle and was not handed over to a noble. Despite this, the only monarch known to have stayed more than the odd night was King Henry III. He had the castle redecorated for his use, with the main hall being repainted so that the stone pillars resembled marble.

Richmond Palace

In about 1299 King Edward I converted the royal manor of Sheen to be a house for his personal use when he wanted to get away from it all with a few friends. Subsequent monarchs made improvements and enlargements until Richard II made it a formal residence as Sheen Palace. This was again enlarged by Henry V, who added a small monastery. The sprawling medieval complex caught fire on 23 December 1497 and was almost entirely razed to the ground.

Henry VII ordered a new palace to be built on the site, giving it the title of Richmond Palace as he had been Earl of Richmond before he became king. The new building was largely completed by 1502 when Henry's daughter Margaret was engaged to James IV of Scotland there in a lavish ceremony. Henry's son, Henry VIII, treated Richmond as a favoured residence and liked to spend Christmas here. His daughter, Queen Mary I, kept her sister Elizabeth at Richmond under house arrest for some months when she was suspected of supporting a Protestant rebellion against Catholic Mary. In her turn Elizabeth came to love Richmond and was a frequent visitor. She died here on 24 March 1603. Thereafter Richmond fell from favour and neither James I nor Charles I spent much time here.

After Charles I was executed, Parliament decided that the nation no longer had much use for royal palaces. Richmond was demolished and the materials sold for £13,000. The Gatehouse remains and is now a private house. Owing to boundary changes, Richmond is now in Greater London.

A view of Richmond Palace as it appeared in about 1630.

3

PLACE NAMES

Abinger
The enclosure belonging to Ebba's people. Unlike most personal names used in place names, Ebba is a woman's name. One famous Ebba was an abbess in Kent who died around the year 680 and became a saint.

Addlestone
The valley belonging to Attel.

Ash Green
The green by the ash trees. In medieval times the ash tree was a profitable if long-term crop. Its combination of strength under compression and fine grain made it ideal for being made into spear shafts.

Ashtead
The place with lots of ash trees.

Bagshot
The land of the badgers.

Banstead
A place where beans are grown.

Bookham
A farmstead with birch trees. Birch wood was long a favourite of carpenters due to its fine grain and decorative patterning. The twigs were used on cooking fires as they burn with a higher temperature than other woods.

Box Hill
A hill on which box trees grow.

Bramley
A thicket of broom. Broom was formerly grown as a crop since its stems and leaves yielded a yellow dye that was especially

effective on woollen cloth. Chemical dyes replaced it in the nineteenth century.

Brockham
The homestead beside a brook.

Burgate
A fortified entrance or gateway.

Burgh Heath
The heath beside the fortified manor house. The word burgh is related to borough and signifies not only a fortified place, but one to which the local militia was expected to rally in times of war. Most of them date to the Viking wars.

Camberley
A name invented in 1877. The place had originated in 1801 as a collection of houses, inns and shops housing the civilian relatives and tradesmen who served the nearby Royal Military College at Sandhurst. By 1810 it was known as 'Cambridge', named after the Duke of Cambridge. When the London & South Western Railway opened a station on a branch line to take advantage of the travellers wanting to reach the college, they at first named the stop 'Cambridge Town'. However, that led to confusion with the university town and to an embarrassing number of parcels ending up in the wrong place. In the end the railway and county authorities decided to ditch the name Cambridge and invented the name Camberley to solve the confusion.

Caterham
The farmstead near the fortified place.

Chertsey
The island belonging to Cerot.

Clandon (East and West)
An open stretch of downland.

Cobham
The farmstead belonging to Cofa. The name Cofa was fairly common in early English times. Another Cofa gave his name to Coventry – a name meaning 'Cofa's Wood'.

Cranleigh
The wood of cranes. The common crane (*Grus grus*) became extinct in England in about 1650, but had been quite commonplace up to that time.

Crowhurst
The wooded hill with crows.

Croydon
The hill of crows.

Dorking
The place belonging to Deorc's people.

Downside
The place beside the hill.

Drakehill
The hill of the dragon. Despite the name there is no legend of a dragon connected to the place – unlike Clandon which has a very lively dragon folktale.

Dunsfold
The grazing enclosure belonging to Dunt.

Durfold
The grazing enclosure where deer are found.

Durrington
The farm belonging to Deora's people.

Effingham
The farmstead belonging to Effa's people.

Egham
The homestead belonging to Ecga.

Elmbridge
The bridge over the misty river.

Elstead
The place with elder trees. The uses of elderflower and elderberries in cookery are widespread and the products delicious.

The bridge at Elstead is over 700 years old, but still carries the main road, the B3001, from Farnham to Godalming. This view was drawn in the 1890s.

Epsom
The homestead belonging to Ebba. This might have been the same Ebba who gave her name to nearby Abinger.

Esher
The place of ash trees.

Ewell
The spring of drinkable water. The spring is still there, supplying the waters that fill the ornamental ponds in the grounds of Bourne Hall. I wouldn't drink the waters these days.

Ewhurst
The copse of yew trees. Yew was used to make longbows, so it was widely planted in medieval times. This name, however, seems to date to pagan days when the yew was considered sacred to the gods.

Frensham
The homestead belonging to Fremi.

Friday Street
The place sacred to the goddess Freya that lies close to a Roman road. The Roman road in question is Stane Street (now the A29 along this section) which connects London to Chichester. Freya was the pagan English goddess of wealth and prosperity. She gave us the weekday Friday.

Frimley
The woodland belonging to Fremi. Presumably this was the same Fremi who gave his name to Frensham.

Godalming
The place belonging to Godhelm's people. This Godhelm was, according to local legend, a fierce and bloodthirsty English pagan warrior. Archaeology has found that the small pre-Roman fort on nearby Hascombe Hill was refortified in about the year 500 or so, then destroyed by fire. Presumably Godhelm was to blame for the bloodshed, after which he settled down in the valley.

Godley
The woodland belonging to Godda.

Guildford
The ford by the golden sand. The ford in question stood just south of the modern town where an outcrop of bright yellow sand occurs beside the River Wey. The ford was dredged out in 1760 when the river was deepened to make it navigable for barges up as far as Godalming.

Hambledon
The crooked hill.

Kingston
The farmstead of the king. The name may also derive from the King's Stone, a boulder that stands just outside the Guildhall. Several kings were crowned when sitting on this stone.

Kingswood
The woodland belonging to Mr King (not to the King of England).

Latchmere
The pool of water in which live leeches. Obviously not a place to go swimming.

Leith Hill
The steep hill.

Lingfield
Open country for people who live in a wood.

Loseley
The clearing in a wood that has a pigsty in it.

Malden Rushett
A hill marked by a cross that lies close to where rushes grow.

Molesey
The island in the River Mole.

Mole, River
Opinion is divided as to whether the river is named from an early English settler named Mul or from the fact that it runs partly underground (like a burrowing mole) for some miles near Leatherhead.

Newark
A new place or new building. The name refers to the priory built here in the 1180s as a new addition to the Augustinian Order.

New Haw
The new grazing enclosure.

Ockham
The farmstead belonging to Occa.

Oxshott
The corner of land belonging to Occa.

Oxted
A place where oaks grow.

Peasmarsh
The marsh where peas grow.

Peper Harow
The pagan temple. The name presumably refers to a survival of worship of the pagan gods into Christian times. The English did not generally build temples to their gods, preferring to worship them in woodland glades, beside lakes or streams and at other natural features. Some have suggested that the name might refer to a ruined Roman temple. No archaeological digs have been carried out here, so the mystery remains unsolved.

Pirbright
The wood of pear trees.

Puttenham
The homestead belonging to Putta.

Redhill
The red hill. This name was invented in 1841 when the London & Brighton Railway Company opened a station in the middle of an empty field to serve as a junction between the main line running north–south from London to Brighton and a second line heading east towards Dover. Because the rocks of the hill through which a tunnel had been bored just to the north were red in colour, the station was named 'Redhill'. The modern town grew up around the isolated railway station in the Victorian period.

Reigate
The gate or opening of the roe deer. The town gained this name in 1088 when William de Warenne, Earl of Surrey, laid out an extensive deer park just to the north, the entrance to which lay close to the town. Before that date it had been known as Cherchefelle, which means 'the open space beside a hill'.

Ripley
A long, thin clearing in a wood.

Runnymede
The meadow where meetings are held. Meetings of the shire court and other public bodies were held here from about 650 onwards and King Alfred the Great held a meeting of his nobles here on at least one occasion. The most famous meeting held here was that of 15 June 1215 when King John affixed his seal to the Magna Carta.

Shalford
The shallow ford. This ford was over the small River Tillingbourne and was shallow in contrast to the ford over the larger River Wey at Guildford.

Stane Street
Stone Roman road. In Old English a 'street' was a Roman road, it has acquired its more modern meaning of a road in a built-up town only because most roads in built-up towns during medieval times were of Roman origin.

Stanwell
The well lined with stone walls. In this context a well might mean a natural spring.

Stoke D'Abernon
The place belonging to the D'Abernon family. The family owned lands around here from the 1080s onwards and rose up the ranks of peerage to become viscounts. The titles and family became extinct in 1941 when the lands and wealth passed to remote cousins.

Stoneleigh
The clearing in the wood where stones are found.

Surrey
The southern region. The name is usually taken to mean that Surrey was an area attached to the Kingdom of the Middle Saxons (Middlesex) which lay to the north. Not much is known about the Middle Saxons and their royal family. The small kingdom had been conquered by the powerful Mercians of the

Midlands by 650 and nobody could be bothered to write down anything about a defeated kingdom except for the fact that it had once existed.

Thames, River
The name seems to be very old and some scholars think that it may be a Celtic corruption of a name that goes back even before the Celts arrived here around 500BC. The word might mean Dark River.

Thunderfield
The open land sacred to Thunor. This Thunor was a god of the pagan English who was the deity of the sky and of weather. He seems to have been associated with farmers and the common people, as opposed to Woden who was associated with warriors and kings. Thunor is today better known as a version of the Viking god Thor, though the two were not identical. He gave us the weekday Thursday.

Thurslea
The clearing sacred to Thunor.

Tilford
The ford belonging to Tila. The village lies at the confluence of the rivers Wey and Slea, with both streams being fordable.

Tuesley
The clearing sacred to Tiw. This pagan English god was a bloodthirsty chap who was worshipped by warriors and seems to have been particularly connected with killing and bloodshed. He gave us the weekday Tuesday.

Walton (on-Thames and on-the-Hill)
The farm belonging to Welsh people. The Welsh referred to here are not immigrants from Wales, but are the original Romano-Britons who lived in Surrey before the English came. The word 'wallas' was originally a fairly derogatory term for foreigners who lived under Roman rule. When the English conquered what is now Surrey, many Romano-Britons stayed on either as slaves, prisoners or free farmers.

Waverley
A wood on or beside marshy ground.

Wey, River
The word wey derives from the Celtic 'uis', meaning simply 'water'.

Weybridge
A bridge over the River Wey. Nobody really knows when the first bridge was built here. It is recorded in the Domesday Book of 1086 and seems to have existed in 850, though that is disputed by some.

Woking
The place belonging to Wocca's people.

Woodmansterne
The thorn tree by the edge of the wood.

4

PEOPLE & CHARACTERS

THE MIGHTY WARENNES

For almost 300 years the richest and most powerful family in Surrey was the Warenne family, who ruled their estates from their great fortress of Reigate Castle. Among the key members of the family were:

William de Warenne
The first William de Warenne came from the little village of Varenne in Normandy. He was a skilled soldier, but an even better administrator who remained loyal to William the Conqueror when that future King of England was a boy facing armed rebellion in Normandy. Warenne fought at the Battle of Hastings and was rewarded with extensive lands. His administrative skills then came to the fore, and he was rewarded by William II, being created Earl of Surrey in 1088 and given even more lands. He died a few months later.

William de Warenne
This William became 2nd Earl of Surrey when his father died in 1088. In about 1093 he asked King Malcolm III of Scotland for the hand of his daughter, Matilda. Malcolm refused and pushed Matilda into an arranged marriage with Henry, the younger son of King William II of England instead. When William II was killed out hunting in the New Forest in 1100, Henry grabbed the crown of England, although his elder brother Robert claimed it for his own. William de Warenne backed Robert, and in response Henry dispossessed him of

his title and estates. In 1103 Robert gave up his claim to the English throne and persuaded Henry to restore William's title of Earl of Surrey, along with his lands. William thereafter was staunchly loyal to Henry and died in 1136. With an interesting lack of imagination he named his son and heir William.

William de Warenne

The third William de Warenne, Earl of Surrey, led a short but adventurous life. He came into his titles in 1136 and was at once plunged into the civil wars of the reign of King Stephen, described in a contemporary chronicle as the 'time when God and his angels slept.' Warenne sided with Stephen, fought at the Battle of Lincoln and led the force that captured Robert, Earl of Gloucester. In 1146 he decided to give up on the civil wars and joined the more noble cause of the Second Crusade. He was killed in a minor skirmish by a Turk on 2 January 1148.

Isabel de Warenne

William the 3rd Earl left all his lands to his only daughter, Isabel, who was not yet married when news of his death came from the Holy Land. King Stephen at once pushed Isabel into marriage with his own son, William of Blois, so that he could drain the Warenne lands of money to help his cause in the civil war. William died in 1159 and Isabel announced that she wanted to marry Count William of Poitou. Because Count William was a cousin of William of Blois, a dispensation to marry was required from the Church. Archbishop Thomas a Becket of Canterbury flatly refused – apparently because the new king, Henry II, supported the marriage. Count William died of a broken heart a few months later at the age of twenty-seven. Young Isabel was made of sterner stuff, however, and in 1164 she married Hamelin, younger brother of Henry II. This marriage lasted forty years and produced four children, the eldest of which was inevitably named William.

William de Warenne

Because Isabel had been Countess of Surrey in her own right, and both her husbands had styled themselves Earl of Surrey, William is generally counted as the 6th Earl of Surrey. He led a generally quiet life, with the only notable incident coming in 1215 when he supported King John against the barons who wanted the king to agree to the Magna Carta. Having lost that dispute, William went back to his estates. He married Maud, daughter of William Marshall, the finest knight and most noble gentleman – though by a long way not the richest – of his generation. In a staggering break with tradition, he named his son and heir John.

John de Warenne

John became 7th Earl of Surrey at the age of just nine. He married Alice de Lusignan, a noble French lady who became astonishingly unpopular in England by constantly telling everyone she met how much nicer everything was in France. John volunteered for the wars in Wales, where he did well playing a large part in the defeat of Llywelyn the Last and the final imposition of English rule in Gwynedd. In 1298 he was called out of retirement by King Edward II to lead a punitive raid into Scotland. The expedition ended in defeat at the Battle of Stirling Bridge, though John did redeem himself by fighting a skilful rearguard action as he retreated back to England. He died in 1304.

John de Warenne

The second John to become Earl of Surrey was the grandson of the 7th Earl, his father having died in 1287. He was one of the leading barons of England during the troubled reign of Edward II. He was one of those who came in for biting satire at the hands of Edward's favourite and lover Piers Gaveston. John de Warenne steered clear of the early disputes, but as Edward's mismanagement of the national governance became clearer he, like others, came to blame the witty, urbane, but heartless Gaveston. In 1311, the nobles of England gathered in rebellion and demanded that Gaveston be sent into exile. Edward refused, so John was sent to capture Gaveston and escort him to France where there were some Gaveston relatives he could live with. John found Gaveston in Scarborough Castle, pledged his word on the Gospels that no harm would be done him and began marching Gaveston south towards London and a ship. They got as far as Deddington in Oxfordshire when they were met by the Earl of Lancaster, the Earl of Warwick and a small army. John was bundled aside, while Lancaster dragged Gaveston from his horse and hacked him to death with a sword. John was furious that his sacred oath had been broken. While Edward collapsed in tears at the death of his boyfriend, John raised his lands in a private war against Lancaster. The feud that followed cost hundreds of lives, brought bloodshed to much of England and ended only when Lancaster was caught red-handed colluding with the Scots. John de Warenne had the satisfaction of sitting in judgement on Lancaster and sending him to his execution. John then fought in the Scottish wars with distinction for some years before retiring to his estates. Although he fathered a number of children, none of them were legitimate.

THE LONELY DUKE

There has only been one Duke of Surrey, and he came to such a sticky end that nobody seems to have wanted to follow him in the title. Thomas Holland was born as the son of the 2nd Earl of Kent in 1374. In 1397 he was summoned by King Richard II and given the task of arresting, for treason, his own uncle, a task he carried out with skill and efficiency. Richard rewarded Thomas by making him Duke of Surrey and bestowing him with rich lands and estates. However, Richard's capricious arrests and executions were soon to prove too much for his subjects to put up with and he was overthrown by his cousin, Henry Bolingbroke, who became King Henry IV. The new king stripped Thomas of his title as Duke of Surrey and of his new estates, but allowed him to keep the lands inherited from his father. Thomas was outraged and began plotting a rebellion with similarly disgruntled men. The rebellion was called for on 4 January 1400 at Kingston in Surrey. Henry was, however, too quick for the rebels and managed to send out messengers summoning an army while he defied the rebels from the walls of London. The rebellion broke up and the leaders scattered. Thomas Holland, one time Duke of Surrey, got as far as Cirencester before he was recognised by men loyal to Henry. He headed for the local abbey hoping to claim sanctuary, but was grabbed from behind, dragged to the town square and beheaded with an axe.

THE HOWARD EARLS

In 1483 the title of Earl of Surrey was recreated for Thomas Howard by Richard III. The Howard Earls were to hold the title down to the present day, but they almost lost it less than two years after they got it.

Thomas Howard

The 1st Earl of Surrey was a loyal man. When Henry Tudor invaded England by way of Wales in 1485, Thomas raised his men and marched to fight alongside Richard III. Surrey took up position on the right wing, but was wounded early in the battle and was carried off for medical treatment. When news arrived that Richard had been killed, Surrey wasted no time in fleeing the vengeance of his enemies. He was, of course, captured later but he had at least escaped the bloody field. Henry demanded that Parliament date the start of his reign from the day before the battle, which would have made Surrey and everyone else in Richard's army guilty of treason. Parliament bravely refused and dated the start of his reign from the day after the battle; Surrey thus escaped execution for treason. When hauled in front of Henry to explain himself, Surrey said that he was always loyal to the King of England, whoever that might be at the time. Surrey was a popular man with many friends, so Henry chose to believe him. Henry was not, however, going to risk having a rich and powerful man living too close to his own estates. He sent Surrey north with orders to watch the Scottish border, hunt down bandits, negotiate with Scottish authorities and generally stay out of the way. Amazingly, Surrey was still there in 1513 when he was aged seventy and a new king, Henry VIII, was on the throne of England. That year Henry went to war with France and King James IV of Scotland took advantage of the situation by invading England with the largest army Scotland had ever mustered. Surrey had the task of meeting the Scots, but with most of the English Army in France he had to rely on levies, militia and the few regular troops stationed in the north. On 9 September Surrey attacked the Scots at Flodden Field and won a resounding victory. King James was killed, as were seven earls, thirty-three lords or clan chiefs, and more knights than anyone could count, plus about 10,000 commoners. The slaughter was terrible. A grateful King Henry promoted Surrey to be the Duke of Norfolk. Since then the title of Earl of Surrey has been held by the eldest son and heir of the Duke of Norfolk.

Henry Howard

The 3rd Earl of Surrey found fame as a poet. He was the first Englishman to write sonnets, and wrote copious blank verse. In January 1547 he was arrested on charges of treason by order of King Henry VIII. Although there was no evidence against him, he was found guilty and executed.

Thomas Howard

The 4th Earl of Surrey spent most of his life fairly quietly, distinguished only by managing to marry in turn three staggeringly wealthy heiresses, each of whom gave him a son before dying suddenly. With his own estates and those he was holding in trust for his sons, he was by 1570 the richest man in England. He was passed over by Queen Elizabeth for any interesting or lucrative government jobs on the grounds that the few tasks he had been given had been bungled. Nevertheless, Thomas Howard had great faith in his own abilities and blamed Elizabeth for his failures. When he was approached in 1571 by Catholic plotters wanting to put Mary Queen of Scots on to the English throne, Howard promptly agreed to join them. He promised to be able to raise 10,000 armed men from his estates, agreed to supervise the execution of Elizabeth and asked in return that he be married to the new queen. This Ridolfi Plot, as it became known, was betrayed to Elizabeth by the Duke of Tuscany who was opposed to Spain – Elizabeth's principal enemy. Howard was arrested and, on 2 June 1572, executed. His titles and estates were forfeited to the Crown.

Thomas Howard

Although reduced to relative poverty by the treason of the 4th Earl, the Howards remained well connected. The 4th Earl's grandson, Thomas Howard, inherited wealth from his mother and in 1604 his maternal uncle persuaded the new King James I to restore the title of Earl of Surrey to the young man. Having perhaps learned from the career of his grandfather, Thomas stayed out of politics and instead spent his time collecting art. When the English Civil War broke out he fled abroad and died in Italy.

THE VISCOUNTS ESHER

In 1885 William Brett – noted lawyer and judge – retired as Master of the Rolls. He was at once raised to the House of Lords with the title of Lord Esher since he had his home in that Surrey village. Brett had earlier had a minor political career which had been marked by the extraordinary election of 1866 in Helston, Cornwall. Brett stood for the Conservatives against Robert Campbell for the Liberals. When the votes were counted, recounted and recounted yet again, there was a tie with both candidates having equal votes. The Mayor of Helston then suggested that he should have the casting vote but although this had some precedence there was no law giving him that power. It was eventually decided that both Brett and Campbell would be declared elected and for the following parliament, Helston had two MPs. A new law was then brought in stating that in the case of a tie in future, the returning officer had to decide who was to be elected by tossing a golden sovereign. Thus, each returning officer at all future elections had to have ready to hand a golden sovereign on election night. This requirement lasted to the constitutional changes brought in by the Labour government of Tony Blair in the twenty-first century. Once in the Lords, Brett proved to be an able legislator and was subsequently promoted to the rank of viscount. Brett was succeeded by his son Reginald, a historian who founded the London Museum. The title is still held by the family, although they no longer live in Esher.

THE VISCOUNTS D'ABERNON

For eleven generations the Vincent family held the title of Baronet of Stoke d'Abernon before they were raised to the peerage. Sir Edgar Vincent, 12th Baronet, spent a lifetime in government service. On one occasion in 1896 he was in

Constantinople when rioting Armenians stormed the bank where he happened to be at the time. Sir Edgar escaped by climbing out through a skylight and fleeing across the rooftops. In 1914 he was appointed Baron d'Abernon and in 1926 was promoted to be Viscount d'Abernon. He married the society beauty Helen Duncombe, but they had no children and the Viscountcy became extinct on his death in 1941.

THE EARLS OF LOVELACE

Based at the lovely Ockham Hall, the King family worked their way up from being seventeenth-century grocers to being Barons of Ockham by the 1830s. In 1838 William King was raised from the rank of Baron to be the Earl of Lovelace. He had married Augusta Byron, daughter of the poet Byron, and between them they made a number of scientific discoveries. The Lovelace family lived at Horsley Towers, built in the mid-nineteenth century by Sir Charles Barry who also built the Houses of Parliament. The construction features a German-style tower and cloisters. The family also built many other buildings around the villages of East and West Horsley. The title is now held by the 5th Earl of Lovelace, a noted naturalist. The family helped to endow Surbiton Grammar School, later to become Esher Grammar School and now Esher College.

THE EARLS OF ONSLOW

Onslow is in Shropshire, but the Onslow family relocated to Surrey in the seventeenth century when they bought Clandon Park, just east of Guildford. The property remained the chief seat of the family until 1956 when it passed to the National Trust. Among the members of the Onslow family have been:

Arthur Onslow

Arthur Onslow served as Speaker of the House of Commons from 1728 to 1761 – an all-time record. His time in office was marked by a reputation for absolute impartiality. In his rulings on procedure and Parliamentary rules he never let himself be swayed by personal feelings, political affiliations or personal advantage. He ferociously protected those MPs who chose to follow an independent course outside the developing system of political parties, ensuring that they had their fair share of speaking time and opportunity to ask questions. The tradition of a speaker being independent of party politics was largely his creation as it had previously been in the gift of the government.

Thomas Onslow, 2nd Earl of Onslow

Holding the earldom from 1814 to 1827, Thomas Onslow was the most famous carriage driver in England. He lived at a time when improving road construction techniques meant that main roads were no longer potholed death traps. He helped to develop the phaeton, a type of carriage with four very large wheels that helped to keep it stable at high speeds. The body of the carriage was very lightly constructed, had only two seats and lacked any space for luggage or other belongings. With his team of four superb black horses, Thomas Onslow set several long-distance records for carriage driving, once famously racing the Prince Regent from London to Brighton and having the audacity to beat his royal friend.

Michael Onslow, 7th Earl of Onslow

The 7th Earl was one of those hereditary peers chosen to remain in the House of Lords when it was partially reformed in 1999. He is the only hereditary peer to have appeared on the satirical TV show *Have I Got News For You*, having done so twice.

THE LORD LIEUTENANTS OF SURREY

The position of Lord Lieutenant is a largely honorary one. The Lord Lieutenant is the monarch's personal representative in a county who carries out various ceremonial functions on behalf of the monarch. Until 1871, the Lord Lieutenant was responsible for the county militia, ensuring there were enough weapons stored locally and that the requisite number of men received basic military training. Presumably the current incumbent (since 1997), Sarah Jane Frances Goad, doesn't have to do too much of that these days.

THE BRAVE

Alfred Vanderbilt

One of the stupendously wealthy American Vanderbilts, who created their fortune from the railroads, Alfred moved to live in South Holmwood after his wife divorced him in scandalous circumstances in 1908. In May 1915 he was returning to England from the USA aboard the passenger liner *Lusitania* when that ship was torpedoed by a German U-boat. The combination of the huge hole blown in the ship by the torpedo and the high speed at which the ship was travelling meant that the ship sank quickly, in less than 18 minutes. As it became clear that there would not be enough time to launch the lifeboats, panic began to grip many passengers. Vanderbilt was instrumental in imposing calm, and ensuring that women and children were put into the few lifeboats that it was possible to launch. At one point he and others physically pushed back men trying to rush the boats. After the last lifeboat had got away, Vanderbilt spotted a young woman clutching a baby. He took off his lifejacket and tied it on to the woman, then helped her over the side of the sinking ship and advised her to swim clear quickly. Vanderbilt was last seen on the deck of the sinking ship as the waves closed around him. He could not swim and his body was never recovered. A monument to his memory stands beside the A24 near to his home.

THE REFORMERS

William Cobbett

Cobbett was born in 1783 in a pub in Bridge Square, Farnham, that has since been renamed in his honour. His father was a poor farmer, so Cobbett joined the army and rose through the ranks to be sergeant major before leaving in 1791. After some years in France and the USA, he founded a newspaper in England in 1800 entitled the *Weekly Political Register*. He used the newspaper to promote radical policies, in particular the abolition of rotten boroughs and other electoral irregularities. In 1810 he was sent to prison after being found guilty of seditious libel, but continued to write and agitate from prison. In 1817 he again went to the USA for two years, returning in 1819 to continue editing his newspaper and agitating for political reform. Among his writings at this time was 'Rural Rides', an account of his travels around England and his opinions of conditions that he found. After electoral reform was enacted he was elected as an MP, a post he held until his death in 1835.

Edward Irving

This Scottish cleric caused a sensation when he began preaching in 1822. His curious blend of passionate oratory, prophetic declarations and charming good looks attracted vast crowds. His actual religious views were very unorthodox and he was put on trial for heresy. He was found not guilty, but lost his living. Henry Drummond of Albury Park remained supportive, and built a church for Irving on the banks of the Tillingbourne. At Albury Park he founded the Holy Catholic Apostolic Church.

Benjamin Brodie

Although born in Wiltshire, surgeon Brodie moved to live at Broome Park at Betchworth so that he could get to London and his more lucrative patients more easily. In 1820 he was elected to the Royal Society and produced a continuous stream of important papers on medical and surgical research. In 1862 he produced his monumental work, *Psychological Inquiries*, which lay down many important principles and described techniques that formed the basis of surgery in the later nineteenth century. His most famous exploit, however, came when the great engineer Isambard Kingdom Brunel accidentally swallowed a penny while performing conjuring tricks for some children. The coin lodged dangerously just above the windpipe meaning that it could have choked Brunel to death at any moment. Brodie devised and built a rotating bed mounted on a wheel so that it could be raised vertically and then turned upside down both gently and carefully. After some manipulation the coin popped out and Brunel was saved.

THE MERCIFUL

In 1644 Sir William Wither of Farnham was captured by the Royalists and, since he had changed sides more than once during the Civil War, was sentenced to the firing squad. However, another Surrey gentleman by the name of Sir John Denham raced to the court to plead for Wither's life and pledged on his own honour that Wither would take no further part in the fighting if his life were to be spared. When the king's judge asked why Denham was so bothered about the life of a traitor, he replied, 'Why, so long as Sir William doth live I am not the worst poet in England.' Sir William's life was indeed spared, though he continued to write some awful verse.

THE HOPEFUL

On 2 May 1687 the parish register of Alfold records that a shilling each was given to Jane Puttock, Henry Manfield and Elizabeth Saker to allow them to travel to London to take part in a 'Touching Ceremony for the King's Evil' to be held later that month by King James II.

The King's Evil was the name then given to the disease now known as scrofula. This is an infection that creates a large, unsightly but painless and harmless growth on the neck below and behind the ear. It was believed that the touch of the monarch could cure, or at least alleviate, the disease. The belief was no doubt encouraged by the fact that the disease did sometimes go into remission. Whether the three villagers of Alfold were cured is not recorded. They would, at least, have come back with a tale to tell of how they met the king and with small silver gilt badges presented by the king himself to prove their tale.

THE FOOL

In 1534 Dr Richard Layton was sent by the government to investigate the state, wealth and condition of Waverley Abbey. His report was scathing.

*The ruined
undercroft
at Waverley
Abbey as it
was in the
1890s.*

Sir,

May it please your mastership to understand that I have
licenced the bringer of this note, the Abbot of Waverley,
to repair unto you for liberty to survey his husbandry
whereupon consisteth the wealth of his monastery. The
man is honest, but none of the children of Solomon. Mr
Treasurer has put servants to him whom the poor fool dare
neither command nor displease. Yesterday, early in the
morning, sitting in my chamber in examination of accounts,
I could neither get bread nor drink, neither fire of these
knaves till I was fretished. And the Abbot durst not speak
to them. I called them all before me and forgot their names,
but took from every man the keys of his office and made
new officers for my time here, perchance as stark knaves as
the others. It shall be expedient for you to give him a lesson
and tell the poor fool what he should do. Among his monks
I found corruption of the worst sort. Thus, I pray God to
preserve you.

Your most assured servant and poor priest,
Richard Layton

5

TRANSPORT
IN SURREY

THE OLD ROADS

Pilgrims' Way

The Pilgrims' Way takes its name from the medieval pilgrims who used it to travel between the great cathedral cities of Winchester and Canterbury. It is, however, much older than that. Archaeological evidence shows that it was in heavy use from about 700BC, and was probably travelled long before that. The way is more of a route than an actual road. It followed the natural causeway formed by the lower slopes of the North Downs that provide easy walking on firm chalk instead of the muddy clay of the Weald to the south or the strenuous climbs and descents of the upper slopes above.

The prehistoric route ran from the port at Folkestone to the sites of Avebury and Stonehenge in Wiltshire – the Canterbury and Winchester spurs became more heavily used in Christian times. From the west, the route enters Surrey at Farnham then heads east to pass south of Guildford, where a medieval spur ran up to the chapel on St Martha's Hill. The Pilgrims' Way then heads east to skirt north of Gomshall, Dorking, Reigate, Merstham, Chaldon, Godstone and Limpsfield, after which it passes out of Surrey into Kent. Parts of the original Pilgrims' Way is now overlain by modern roads, so the long-distance footpath bypasses these sections to remain on unsurfaced tracks.

Stane Street

The main Roman road in Surrey is Stane Street which ran from London to Chichester (Noviomagus Reginorum to the Romans) – a distance of some 56 miles. The road was of standard Roman construction for a rural road in the provinces. It was flanked by drainage ditches 84ft apart. A strip 24ft wide was covered first with sand or gravel that was compacted down. Over this was a layer of sandstone pebbles (flint nodules from up on the downs), over which was another layer of compacted gravel. These layers added up to about 11 inches in all and there was a camber to throw rainwater off into the ditches. The road was built in about AD 60 and was maintained to a high level until about 380 when regular repair and maintenance seems to have stopped. For much of its route in Surrey, Stane Street is followed by the A24 or the A29, though some sections on the downs have been abandoned and now show up as humps in the grassy turf.

The Brighton Way

A secondary Roman road turned off Stane Street at Kempton and headed south to reach the South Coast close to where Portslade now stands. In Surrey it runs through Caterham, Godstone and Felbridge, though the precise route is not always known. The date of construction is also not known, but it seems to have been linked to the development of the iron industry in the Weald, which began in about AD 120. The route remained in use during the earliest English period, as village names such as Streatham, Stanstead and Stratton all derive from terms for a surfaced road, but by the 900s it seems to have fallen out of use along most of its length and was forgotten by later medieval times. Only in a few places do modern roads follow this route – the B2235 through Godstone and the Tilburstow Hill Road north of Blindley Heath, for instance.

The Lewes Road

The Romans built a road from London to Lewes. Near Tatsfield the course of the road forms the boundary between Surrey and

Kent for some miles. The route of the road then skirts east of Limpsfield before entering Kent where the B2036 runs along its route for a while. The Roman villa, fulling workshops and possible temple at Titsey were found just to the west of this road.

NAVIGATION CANALS

The Mole

In 1664 Parliament passed an act that allowed for the Mole to be made navigable from Reigate to the Thames. Although some surveying work was carried out, nothing was actually achieved. A rather more modest scheme was suggested in 1798 that was to link chalk quarries near Betchworth to works at Dorking by way of a canalised stretch of the Mole – but again nothing came of the plan. The dangers posed by French warships to merchantmen going up the Channel to reach London led to the proposal to build a canal from Portsmouth to Chatham so that the ships could dock in Portsmouth and unload their cargoes to barges to be moved to the Thames Estuary and so avoid the most perilous part of the journey. A branch of this canal was to go down the Mole, which was to be made navigable along most of its course. However, the Royal Navy proved to be so effective that the scheme never went ahead. An even more ambitious plan to build a canal wide enough to take the merchant ships themselves was proposed in 1820. It was to go up the Mole to near Reigate, then strike across country to Chichester. However, the company could not attract enough money to build the canal and the idea was shelved. The Mole was never made navigable for canal barges, with only the 500 yards or so closest to the Thames being able to handle craft this large. However, it has been used by locals in rowing boats for fishing and other purposes for centuries.

The Wey Navigation Canal

The River Wey had been used by small boats since prehistoric times, but it was in 1635 that Sir Richard Weston had the idea of making it navigable to large barges. Weston had spent much of his youth in the Netherlands, so when he inherited the family estates near Guildford it was only natural that he should think of Dutch methods to improve his income. His original plan was to improve the Wey by deepening shallows, cutting off long bends and inserting locks to maintain water depth on the stretch from Weybridge to Guildford. He would then operate barges from Guildford down the Wey to the Thames and thus on to London. This would increase the market for goods from his own estates and those of his neighbours. Work was interrupted by the English Civil War, but was completed by 1651. In 1764 the improvements were continued upstream to reach Godalming. Unlike many canals, the Wey Navigation Canal did not suffer unduly from the building of the railways. It is still in use today, albeit mostly for pleasure craft.

The Wey and Arun Junction Canal

In 1810 the Earl of Egremont had the idea of linking the Wey Navigation Canal in Surrey to the similar Arun Navigation Canal in Sussex, thus providing a route for barges from the English Channel to the Thames. Egremont used his contacts to get permission for the work, raised the £86,000 needed and construction was completed in 1816. The canal did well, not only transporting goods between the Thames and the Channel but also moving goods in and out of the areas through which it ran. However, in 1865 a railway opened from Guildford to Horsham, in direct competition to the canal. The railway provided transport that was faster and cheaper, so the canal could not compete. It closed in 1871 and fell into disrepair. In the early twenty-first century efforts began to reopen the canal for pleasure boat use.

SURREY RAILWAYS

Banstead & Epsom Downs Railway

Founded in 1863 to promote a branch line from Sutton to the Epsom Downs racecourse, the Banstead & Epsom Downs Railway was short lived. The company received Parliamentary permission for the line, surveyed the route and demonstrated the financial profits that could be made from the line. The company then sold out to the LB&SCR earning a tidy profit for its shareholders. The line still exists, although it was shortened slightly in the 1980s to allow the site of the original Epsom Downs station to be sold for housing development.

British Railways (BR)

The nationalised railway of Britain was created in 1948. In Surrey the Southern Railway became the Southern Region of BR. Although BR rebuilt many stations and bridges in Surrey, the only major change to the rail network came in 1965 when the Guildford to Horsham line via Bramley and Cranleigh was closed. In 1997 BR was split up and privatised. Track became the property of Railtrack, while the operation of train services was divided between a number of companies.

Caterham Railway Company (CRC)

The village of Caterham was a sleepy little place until 1856 when the CRC finished building a line from Caterham to Purley, where it linked to the LB&SCR. There was plenty of available building land and it was hoped that houses for commuters working in London would be built, providing passenger traffic for the railway. Unfortunately, Caterham lay in the area that the LB&SCR and SER had agreed belonged to the SER. With a mainline connection with the LB&SCR, the Caterham line fell between two stools. Neither the SER nor the LB&SCR wanted anything to do with the line, and their opposition dissuaded property developers from building houses. In 1859 the Caterham Railway Company went bankrupt and was bought out by the SER. It was not until the 1890s that the hoped-for housing developments began.

Croydon, Merstham & Godstone Iron Railway

Formed in 1803 the Croydon, Merstham & Godstone Iron Railway was intended to run from Croydon to Reigate with a branch to Godstone Green. It was never completed, stopping at Merstham. The line served the quarries where hearthstones were made and chalk extracted to be made into lime. As a secondary business horse manure was brought from London for the use of Surrey farmers. Unlike later railways, the Croydon, Merstham & Godstone Iron Railway used horse-drawn wagons. In 1837 it was bought out by the London Brighton Railway.

Epsom & Leatherhead Railway (ELR)

Formed in 1856 the ELR built a single line from Leatherhead via Ashtead to the LB&SCR station at Epsom. The line opened in 1859, but the ELR never actually operated it. Instead the company made its money by renting the line to the LB&SCR who operated the trains. In 1865 the LB&SCR made a cash offer to buy out the ELR, which was accepted.

Great Cockrow Railway

Built in 1968 and privately owned, the Great Cockrow Railway runs on a 7¼in gauge track through private woodland west of Chertsey. It is open on Sundays through the summer, offering passenger rides on miniature steam trains to the public.

Guildford Junction Railway

This company was formed by a group of Guildford businessmen who wanted to bring the railway to Guildford in order to improve transport links for their town. The company surveyed a route from the LSWR station in Woking and hired William Prosser to construct the route. The LSWR, however, announced it would prefer to build the line itself and made the shareholders of the Guildford Junction an offer that they chose to accept. The new line opened on 5 May 1845.

Guildford, Kingston & London Railway (GKLR)

The GKLR was a strange company born in 1881 out of the desires of a mixed bag of investors. Among these was the successful Metropolitan District Railway, running what is now the Metropolitan Line of the London Underground, which wanted to extend its line south of the Thames. The town councils of Kingston and Guildford were unhappy with being served only by small branch lines. The wealthy Earl of Onslow, Lord Lovelace and Lord Foley, meanwhile, owned extensive tracts of Surrey countryside that were not served by railways at all. Together they cooked up a scheme to extend the Metropolitan Railway from Putney through Kingston and Thames Ditton and thence south-west through Claygate, Cobham, Horsley and Clandon to Guildford. Branch lines to Ashtead and Bookham were included in the proposed railway. Not wanting the Metropolitan to become a rival in what it viewed as its own territory, the LSWR approached the GKLR with a proposal to build and operate the sections of line south of Thames Ditton. The lords and Guildford Council jumped at the offer, with the Metropolitan and Kingston being left out in the cold. The new LSWR line to Guildford via Claygate, Clandon (and stops in between) opened in 1885.

Horsham & Guildford Direct Railway

This supposedly independent railway company was little more than a front organisation for the LB&SCR. The route linked the LSWR station at Guildford to the LB&SCR

station at Horsham, a distance of 16 miles. At first the LSWR welcomed the line as it thought it would bring extra traffic to its line from London to Portsmouth via Guildford. Once it realised that a major shareholder in the new company was the LB&SCR, however, the LSWR announced it would not allow the new line to use its station. The LB&SCR then went public with its involvement and announced plans for its own Guildford station. The LSWR then relented and gave the new line permission to use the existing station. The line opened in 1865.

Horsham, Dorking & Leatherhead Railway (HDLR)

Founded in 1862 by landowners in the area over which the railway was to run, the HDLR modelled itself on the ELR. The HDLR intended to build and own the line, but to have the LB&SCR run the actual services. In 1864 the LB&SCR announced that it would rather own the line outright, and bought out the HDLR. The investors made a profit and got the railway line that they wanted.

London & Southampton Railway (LSR)

Founded in 1834 to link the two cities named in its title, the LSR had its London terminal beside docks on the Thames at Nine Elms – now Vauxhall station. It opened as far as Woking in May 1838 and to Shapley in September that same year. By 1839 the line had reached Basingstoke and Winchester in 1840 with the through line completed later that year. No sooner was the line completed than the company began works on lines to Salisbury, Dorchester, Weymouth, Windsor, Reading and Godalming. Clearly the name London & Southampton Railway was no longer good enough, so it was changed to the London & South Western Railway in 1840.

London and Brighton Railway (LBR)

This company was founded in 1837 to build a line from London to Brighton, with a branch to Shoreham. The line was completed in 1841. In Surrey the railway ran south through Merstham and Horley, with a tunnel through the downs at Merstham that was one of the longest in the world when it was built. A station was put in an empty field beside a lane leading to Reigate and named Redhill, owing to the colour of the rocks. The town of Redhill grew from that station. The line proved to be popular and profitable. In 1846 the LBR merged with the London & Chichester Railway, the Brighton & Chichester Railway and the Brighton, Lewes & Hastings Railway to form the London, Brighton & South Coast Railway.

London, Brighton & South Coast Railway (LB&SCR)

In 1860 the new LB&SCR built a bridge over the Thames and constructed a grand new terminus at London Victoria, still the London end of the network. The company also built or took over new lines in Surrey, including those to Epsom Downs, Leatherhead, Dorking, Guildford, Oxted and Cranleigh. Most of the company's expansion was, however, in Sussex or south London.

In the wake of the First World War it was realised that the railways had been heavily overused and required massive investment. Many of the smaller companies were unable to raise the capital and faced closure. In 1923 the government decided to force a series of massive mergers on the railway companies so that the profitable lines would take over those in financial difficulties. The LB&SCR became part of the Southern Railway.

London & South Western Railway (LSWR)

When the LSR became the LSWR one of its first acts was to move its London terminus closer to the City. In 1845 work began on a line from Vauxhall to London Bridge with an intermediate station at Waterloo Bridge. The line opened as far as Waterloo Bridge in 1848, but the rest of the route to London Bridge was never completed. The London terminus came to be at Waterloo Bridge, later renamed just Waterloo.

Meanwhile, works in Surrey continued. The LSWR came to operate trains on several lines in Surrey in addition to the main London–Southampton line through Surbiton, Woking and Farnborough. The line from Woking to Portsmouth via Guildford and Godalming, the line from Surbiton through Claygate and Clandon to Guildford and the Shepperton branch were all run by the LSWR. In the 1923 reorganisation, the LSWR became part of the Southern Railway.

Portsmouth Railway

In 1858 a group of Portsmouth businessmen formed the Portsmouth Railway Company and built a line from Havant to the LSWR station at Godalming. The LSWR agreed to operate trains over the new line and services began in 1859. The LSWR wanted the Portsmouth Railway to extend the line into Portsmouth itself, but soon found that the necessary land was owned by the LB&SCR, which refused to sell. Complex negotiations ensued between the LSWR, LB&SCR and the SER which resulted in the Portsmouth Railway being allowed to use the SER Portsmouth terminus. In 1877 the Portsmouth Railway was bought out by the LSWR.

Reading, Guildford & Reigate Railway (RGRR)

Founded by Guildford banker Frederick Mangles, the RGRR completed a line between the three named towns in 1849. During the course of construction, the RGRR had approached the three big railways in Surrey asking how much they would pay to operate trains over the lines. The SER made the highest offer and began running trains in 1850. Two years later the SER bought out the RGRR.

South Eastern Railway (SER)

The SER was always primarily a Kent railway company. In Surrey it ran the east–west line that ran through Guildford, Dorking, Redhill and Godstone. In the 1923 reorganisation, the SER became part of the Southern Railway.

Southern Heights Light Railway

Founded in 1925 to build a light rail line from the main line station at Sanderstead over the downs to Orpington in Kent, it was hoped that this electrified line would open up the area to residential development. The company was still in the process of planning its route when the stock market crash of 1929 struck and the SHLR went bankrupt.

Southern Railway (SR)

The Southern Railway was formed in 1923 by an amalgamation of the SER, LB&SCR, LSWR and a number of smaller companies. It operated all the railways in Surrey, introducing electrification to suburban lines while retaining steam for the long-distance trains. The only new line built by the company in Surrey was the branch line to Chessington South from Raynes Park with intermediate stations at Motspur Park, Malden Manor, Tolworth and Chessington North. It was originally planned to extend the line to Leatherhead, but the outbreak of war in 1939 halted work and it was never restarted. In 1948 the Southern Railway was nationalised to become the Southern Region of British Railways.

Staines & West Drayton Railway

In 1885 this small company built a line from Staines through Colnbrook to West Drayton and leased out the right to run trains over the line to the Great Western Railway (GWR). The arrangement lasted until 1900 when the GWR bought out the smaller company.

Staines, Wokingham & Woking Junction Railway

This railway company was ambitiously named since its lines never got as far as Woking. The Staines to Wokingham section was leased in 1856 to the SER, which later bought out the smaller company.

Sunningdale & Cambridge Town Railway

Although an independent company, this railway was backed by the army which wanted a line linking the staff college at Cambridge Town (now Camberley) and the huge camp and practice grounds at Aldershot to the main railway network. The company began work in 1864, but in 1866 the investors decided that the anticipated army traffic would not be enough to turn a profit. The work was stopped and the company folded.

Surrey & Sussex Junction Railway (SSJR)

Founded in 1865 this company was a front for the LB&SCR that wanted to promote a line from Croydon to Tunbridge Wells via Oxted that would stop the SER from using the route. The work on the line was only ever half-hearted as the cuttings, viaducts and tunnels were always going to be expensive and anticipated traffic was low. In 1869 the LB&SCR took over the SSJR and stopped work on the line. It would be 20 years before the line was built.

Surrey Border & Camberley Railway

This light railway ran from Camberley to Frimley and opened in 1938. The outbreak of war in 1939 doomed the company, which folded in 1941.

Thames Valley Railway (TVR)

In 1860 W.S. Lindsay, Lord of the Manor at Shepperton, founded this company with the intention of linking Shepperton to the LSWR main line at Twickenham. The LSWR agreed to operate the trains, which first ran in 1864. The line proved to be a huge success and soon it was obvious that the single track could not handle the traffic. The TVR could not raise the capital to install a twin track, so the LSWR bought out the small company and did the work itself.

CANAL MEETS RAILWAY

In 1794 the Basingstoke Canal was completed, linking that town with the Thames via the Wey. When Parliament began debating the construction of a proposed railway from London to Southampton, the Basingstoke Canal company realised that the railway would not only take custom away from their waterway, but would also cut across their route. They successfully lobbied Parliament to insert into the railway bill a clause stating that the railway must not interrupt the use of the canal. The railway company, the London & South Western Railway (LSWR), solved this problem by ingeniously working around the canal. At Frimley Green the most impressive engineering feat can be seen from the B3012 just south of the village. A four-arch aqueduct carries the canal over the railway. It is not everywhere you can see a boat going over a train!

THREE MOST POPULAR
STREET NAMES IN SURREY

High Street	86
Church Road	70
Station Road	63

SURREY EXTREMES

Most northerly point:
> Junction of Priest Hill and Windsor Road, north of Englefield Green

Most westerly point:
> Wimble Hill, about 2 miles west of Farnham

Most southerly point:
> Chase Warren Wood, off Tennyson's Lane south of Haslemere.

Most easterly point:
> Crockham Hill, off Kent Hatch Road just east of Limpsfield Chart

Highest Point:
> Summit of Leith Hill 965ft (294m) above sea level

Lowest Point:
> North end of Ferry Road, Thames Ditton 31ft (9.5m) above sea level

6

BUSINESS & LEISURE

INDUSTRIAL HISTORY

Treadmill Crane

From at least 200 BC the standard method of lifting heavy
weights on building sites or at docks was by way of a
treadmill crane. A donkey or luckless human was put in the
treadmill and set walking in order to pull on a rope that was
attached by pulleys to the weight to be lifted. Unsurprisingly
the advent of steam power, followed by electrical power and
internal combustion, marked the end of the old treadmill
crane – except in Guildford. Installed in about 1680 to lift
cargo out of canal boats on to the dock at the bottom end of
Friary Street, the treadmill crane continued in use until 1960.
It then became redundant when the dock was closed. In 1970
the redevelopment of the Friary Centre meant that the crane
had to be moved. It is now a Grade I Listed monument and
stands on the banks of the Wey beside the bridge.

Roman Tile Factory

In about AD 150 a factory producing roofing tiles was opened
at Ashtead as part of a villa complex that seems to have
been linked to Stane Street, a road running from London to
Chichester. The huge pit from which the Romans dug out the
clay for the factory can still be seen on Ashtead Common,
though it is now rather overgrown by trees.

The Wealden Iron Industry

From Roman times to the eighteenth century southern Surrey
was an important centre for the iron industry. Deposits of iron
ore in the nearby hills, combined with plentiful supplies of

charcoal from the forests that grew on the clay soil provided the raw materials. The Tillingbourne stream was dammed in several places to provide the motive power for the great hammers which pounded the iron as it was shaped. Several of these hammer ponds can be seen between Shere and Wotton. In Abinger Hammer, named after the hammers that used to work here, there is a nineteenth-century clock hanging over the A25 which features an automated blacksmith with a great hammer who strikes a bell on the hour.

The Old Glass Industry

Before the advent of industrialisation, the process of glass manufacture needed ample supplies of charcoal, limestone and the correct sort of sand. All three were to be found in south-western Surrey and so the area became a centre for the English glass industry. Chiddingfold glass was particularly highly rated. It was used in St George's Chapel, Windsor, and in St Stephen's, Westminster.

The oldest record of a glassworks here is from the thirteenth century, though glass may have been made here in earlier times. By the 1580s there were eleven glassworks overlooking the village green alone. Most of these have been swept away by subsequent rebuilding, but remains of the industry can be found. There is a plaque in the church, several of the windows of which were made locally. South of the village in Highbeech Wood can be found the tumbled ruins of one of the largest and latest glassworks. There is a footpath running into the woods from Pickhurst Road, near Gales Farm. Glass was also made at Alford. In the sixteenth century the French master craftsman Jean Le Carré moved to Alford, using charcoal from the local woods to fire his furnace.

WINDMILLS IN SURREY

Ewhurst Windmill is a four-storey brick tower mill that was built in 1840. It has recently been converted into a house and is now private property.

Outwood Windmill is the oldest working windmill in England. It was built in 1665 by Thomas Budgen, whose family owned it until 1806 when the Jupp family took over and ran it until 1962 when the Thomas family bought it. The mill is a post mill standing on a single-storey round house, the structure is mostly built of oak. In 1796 a much larger smock mill was built next door, but it collapsed in high winds in 1960.

Buckland Windmill does not grind grain, it is a sawmill. This smock mill was built for the use of the Buckland Court Estate in the 1860s and by the 1940s had fallen out of use. It was restored in the 1990s and is now in working order.

The Lowfield Heath Mill at Charlwood was built in about 1762 and remained in operation until 1880. It is a 20ft diameter post mill on a single-storey roundhouse. Restoration work began in the 1980s and it was restored to working order in 1997.

Frimley Green Windmill was constructed as a four-storey brick tower mill in 1784. It ceased operation in the 1890s and has now been converted to a private house.

Reigate Heath Windmill was built in about 1760 as a post mill on a single-storey roundhouse. It ceased operation in 1862 and was converted into a chapel attached to Reigate parish. An interesting fact about this building is that it is the only windmill in the world that has been consecrated as a place of worship. In 2003 it was restored by Reigate Borough Council.

Tadworth New Mill was built in about 1762, though a windmill has been on the site since 1295 – the oldest in southern England. It remained in operation until 1902. In 1940 a German bomber scored a near miss that caused damage, and a V1 came down nearby in 1944 causing more damage. The structure is a post mill on a two-storey roundhouse.

Wray Common Windmill was built as a five-storey brick tower mill in 1824. It remained in operation until 1928 when it was converted to be a residential house. In 2004 the cap and sails were replaced to restore the external appearance to that of a windmill, though the interior remains a house.

RACECOURSES

Sandown Park

The racecourse at Sandown, just outside Esher, was a world first. All other racecourses at the time were on common land and were entirely open to anyone who turned up. No set course was laid out and races tended to be run between two fixed points, with riders choosing their route and the crowd getting in the way. There were constant problems with drunkenness, pick-pocketing and other undesirable activities. So when the Church of England offered a long lease on its farmland at Sandown, it was snapped up by a group of sporting gentlemen who wanted to effect change. Their idea was to lay out a racecourse on private land, surrounded by a fence and then charge admission to the course. In that way they could not only keep out undesirables, but also raise money to pay for luxurious facilities such as a grandstand and toilets. The Sandown Park racecourse was opened in 1875 and although the first meeting was slightly marred by heavy rain, the concept proved a big hit. Middle class folk came from London in vast numbers, using Esher railway station next to the course, attracted by the safety and the facilities. The Church of England, however, was unimpressed and decided it did not want to earn money through gambling. They sold the land. Sandown has never looked back and continues to offer luxurious facilities to the race-going public.

Kempton Park

The fact that Sandown was an immediate success was noticed by businessman S.H. Hyde, who owned Kempton Manor near Sunbury. The grounds had the same features as Sandown – proximity to a railway station and relatively flat land. Hyde laid out a racecourse and opened it in July 1878. It has been open ever since, with the most famous race being the King George VI Chase held every Boxing Day. The legendary racehorse Desert Orchid won the race on no fewer than four occasions. In 2006, Kempton Park was given a new all-weather Polytrack synthetic surface and floodlighting to facilitate racing in all conditions and at all light levels.

Lingfield Park

So successful was the concept of a 'park racecourse', that in 1890 a third such course was opened in Surrey at Lingfield. The racecourse was located in a 450-acre estate and at first held jump racing only, but in 1894 flat racing began. In 1987 a golf course was developed inside the race track, again as at Sandown. In 2004, £5.5 million was spent on a new grandstand that included conference and banqueting facilities.

Hurst Park

A fourth park racecourse was laid out at Hurst Park, a short walk from the Hampton Court railway station at West Molesey, Surrey. The Triumph Hurdle was run here from 1939. The course closed in 1962 and most of the site has now been developed as housing.

Epsom Downs

Meanwhile, Surrey's oldest racecourse continued to thrive despite the competition from the new style of park racecourses. The first recorded race was held on the downs in 1661, although the accounts make it clear that horse racing had been taking place for many decades before that date. Indeed, it is thought that King James I had attended racing on the downs when staying at nearby Nonsuch Palace. In those days there was no set course. Races were held from various points across the downs to a finishing post erected somewhere near the site of the current grandstand. The pub in Banstead High Street was a favoured starting point, though longer races from more distant places were also run.

By the late eighteenth century actual routes for the races were being laid out in an attempt to keep the large crowds out of the way of the horses. In 1780 Edward Smith-Stanley, 12th Earl of Derby, organised a race for him and his friends to race their three-year-old fillies. He named it the Oaks after his estate. At a celebratory dinner after the race the idea of a race for colts and fillies was suggested, apparently by Sir Charles Bunbury who was Steward of the Jockey Club and Derby agreed to organise it. A dispute then arose as to whether the new race should be called the Bunbury or the Derby, the issue being settled by the toss of a coin. Thus the Derby was first run the following year – and was won by a horse owned by Bunbury.

Since then the racecourse has undergone a number of changes, most recently with a new grandstand opening in 2009. The course remains laid out on common land and it is still possible for anyone to turn up to watch the races for free – though you would have to get there early in the day to watch the Derby from a good vantage point.

7

RELIGION

FIVE BRONZE AGE BURIAL BARROWS

Crooksbury Common, Elstead. Three bell barrows.
Frensham Common, Frensham. Four bowl barrows.
Horsell Common, Woking. Two bell barrows.
Newlands Corner, near Shere. Single round barrow.
Whitmore Common, Worplesdon. Two bell barrows.

RUINED CHURCHES

St Catherine's Chapel stands on a hill overlooking the Wey just
south of Guildford. It was built in 1301 on the site of an earlier
chapel dedicated to St Catherine that had fallen into disrepair.
An annual fair was held around the chapel from 1308 to 1914,
and was painted by J.M.W. Turner. The chapel fell into ruins
about the time of the Reformation, but locals kept it patched
up as a scenic ruin and landmark.

*St Catherine's
Chapel, just
south of
Guildford,
now stands in
ruins.*

MEGALITHS

The great standing stones of Stonehenge, Avebury and elsewhere date back to the Bronze Age when circles and lines of gigantic standing stones were erected across much of north-western Europe. There are only two megaliths known from Surrey, and both have unnerving legends associated with them.

The Pyrford Stone stands at the junction of Upshott Lane and Pyford Common Road, close to the aptly named Stone Farm. It has long been said locally that at midnight on nights of the full moon, the stone will lift itself up out of the ground and move around the area before returning to its place. Until 1976 the stone stood in the angle of the junction, which seriously restricted the width of the road. The new articulated lorries coming into use by the 1970s simply could not get around the tight corner so the stone was uprooted and moved to the outside of the bend, with the road being considerably widened at the same time. Locals muttered that no good would come of moving the stone, but the council ignored such superstitious twaddle. Since then the stone would seem to have exacted a revenge. The junction may now be wider and less angled than it was, but it would seem to have become strangely more dangerous. On frosty mornings when a mist creeps up from the River Wey, something odd seems to happen here. Car drivers are unable to judge the distances properly and a disturbing number of them end up in the ditch. Such accidents rarely lead to injury and nobody has been killed – yet.

The second megalith used to stand beside the ford on the Reigate Road over the Shag Brook just east of Buckland. According to local legend the Shag Stone was the lair of a hideous, hairy monster which took the form of a deformed human with glaring red eyes and savage talons. This monster lay in wait beside the stream, ready to leap out and attack any traveller who did not pay proper respects to the stone and its supernatural guardian.

In 1816 one local boy back from the Napoleonic Wars volunteered to ride over the ford at midnight when a full moon bathed the area – generally held to be the most dangerous time to try the feat. He set off on his horse, and came back considerably more quickly than he had set off. He said that he had crossed the ford, but never went that way again after dark. This tale would appear to be a dimly remembered echo of a pagan reality. The stone may well have been dedicated to some pagan deity, the juxtaposition of a ford and a standing stone is highly significant. Even more so is the name of the Shag Brook. A shag is an Old English word usually translated as 'demon', but it had a more specific meaning of a non-Christian spirit or deity.

The ford was changed into a bridge in the mid-nineteenth century. The local vicar took the opportunity of the presence a gang of tough workmen from outside the area to have the Shag Stone removed. No local man would dare undertake such a task. Unlike at Pyford, the destruction of the Shag Stone would seem to have sorted out the problem as there has been no trouble since.

PAGAN TEMPLES

The only pagan temple so far firmly identified in Surrey stood on a hilltop on Farley Heath. It was erected in the very earliest days of the Roman occupation of Britain, in about AD 70, and remained in use until destroyed by fire in about 450, a time when the English were invading. A road linked the temple to Stane Street, so it must have been of more than simply local importance. The site was excavated by Martin Tupper in the nineteenth century who found much Roman material, but nothing to indicate to which deity the temple was dedicated. The finds are now in the British Museum, while the outlines of the fallen walls are picked out in concrete on the site. The site is now in a wood and can be approached via a footpath off Farley Heath Road, east of the village.

There may have been a temple at Ashtead. This was a large and prosperous place in Roman times, though since most of the site is now built over, it is impossible to excavate to find out much detail. The medieval church is surrounded by earthworks and stands adjacent to Stane Street, the old Roman road. It has been suggested that it occupies the site of a Roman temple, the earliest Christian missionaries often preached on pagan sites to demonstrate the power of the Christian god and there are many Roman bricks and tiles reused in the Church walls.

At Titsey there was a small cluster of Roman workshops that seem to have been used to full wool produced on the nearby downs. A small, rectangular building with a colonnade has been interpreted as being a shrine.

CHURCHES DEDICATED TO ST MARY

St Mary, also known as the Virgin Mary, was the mother of Jesus Christ. The dedication of a church to St Mary usually indicates a date of between 1100 and 1400. Before that date churches tended to be dedicated to local saints or to major figures such as Christ, St Paul or St Peter. After that date few new churches were built in Surrey and with the Protestant Reformation of the sixteenth century the special veneration of the Virgin Mary faded away. In Surrey the following parish churches are dedicated to St Mary:

Bletchingley
Chiddingfold
Dunsfold
Farleigh
Fetcham
Guildford

Oxted
Stanwell
Stoke D'Abernon
Tatsfield
Thorpe
West Horsley

At Littleton and Reigate the churches are dedicated to a different St Mary – St Mary Magdalene. This Mary is a rather enigmatic figure who seems to have been a leading member of Christ's followers but is not numbered among the Apostles.

Oxted Church is one of many in Surrey dedicated to St Mary.

SAXON CHURCHES IN SURREY

The north wall at Albury and the lower sections of the tower are pre-1066, though the rest of the church was rebuilt in the thirteenth century.

The bell tower of the Church of St Nicholas at Compton is pre-Norman in date. The rest of the church was added in about 1140.

Parts of St Mary's, Fetcham, were built with reused Roman bricks and tiles and are thought to date back to about 950.

The southern half of St Mary's, Stoke D'Abernon, is thought to be Saxon in date.

NORMAN CHURCHES IN SURREY

The south arcade at Alfold is of Norman date.

The main tower at Betchworth is almost Norman in date. It was built in Norman times, but in 1851 began to crumble. It was taken down and rebuilt, stone by stone, exactly as it had been originally.

Bletchingley has a massive Norman tower.

St Lawrence's in Caterham is largely of Norman work.

Chaldon's Church of St Peter and St Paul is largely Norman, but larger windows were added in medieval times. It has a rare *c.* 1200 painting of the Ladder of Redemption and the Pit of Hell.

Charlwood boasts the Church of St Nicholas, which dates back to 1080 and has a fine crown post roof.

Pyrford's Church of St Nicholas is almost unaltered since the major renovations carried out in 1198. The only significant change since then was the installation of pews in the 1480s.
The nave of Tatsfield church is Norman, with rare surviving Norman windows. The rest of the church is thirteenth-century.

MODERN CHURCHES IN SURREY

Camberley boomed in population after the railway arrived in Victorian times. In 1907 a new parish was created, so a brick and timber church was erected.

Caterham's St Mary's was built in Victorian times as the population increased rapidly after the arrival of the railway. It replaced the much smaller and older St Lawrence's.

Overlooking Esher Green is Christ Church, built in 1854 since the older church on the hill was too small for the village's growing population.

The Church of St Peter was rebuilt in Victorian times, with only the fifteenth-century tower remaining of the original.

The Cathedral of the Holy Spirit, Guildford. This huge church was completed in 1961 to serve the diocese of Guildford, created in 1927. It was built in a modern version of medieval Gothic with greatly simplified lines and soaring vaulting. The tower is 160ft high and is topped by a 15ft golden angel weathervane, which now doubles up as a mobile phone mast. The bricks out of which it is built were made on-site from the clay on which it stands.

Hascombe's Church of St Peter was built in the 1860s. It has some of the finest Victorian stained glass in the country.

The church of the Wisdom of God in Lower Kingswood was completed in 1891 in sumptuous style including coloured and patterned stone from as far afield as Turkey.

The Church of St Mark in Whiteley Village was built in 1919 to mimic the restrained Gothic of the early fourteenth century.

CHURCHES DEDICATED TO ST GEORGE

The patron saint of England has been St George since about 1250 – before that date England seems to have been the preserve of St Edmund, a king of East Anglia butchered by pagan Vikings in 869. Perhaps a victorious dragon-slayer had rather more appeal than a king who lost both his life and kingdom to the enemy! In Surrey the following churches are dedicated to St George:

Ashtead
Badshot Lea
Crowhurst
Esher – the older of the two churches
West End – in reality a chapel for the Claremont Estate

MONASTIC CENTRES IN SURREY

Chertsey Abbey, Benedictine

Founded in 666 by Erkenwald, a Mercian nobleman who also founded Barking Abbey. Erkenwald was appointed the first abbot at Chertsey and went on to become Bishop of London and to advise King Ine of Wessex in the compilation of a law code for that kingdom. He died in 693 and was buried in St Paul's Cathedral – though his tomb was destroyed in the Great Fire of London in 1666, exactly 1,000 years after he founded Chertsey Abbey. The abbey grew to be the biggest and richest in Surrey. It was destroyed by the pagan Vikings, then refounded and once again rose to great heights of wealth and learning. It was closed in 1538.

Esher Hospital

The Hospital of the Holy Ghost at Sandon was dedicated to the Holy Spirit by the founder Robert de Wateville in about 1160. It was always a small house and in 1249 all twelve brethren were wiped out by the Black Death. It was refounded, but in 1436 the hospital was found to be in serious financial difficulties due to unspecified 'improper acts and administrations'. It was merged with the Hospital of St Thomas the Martyr at Southwark, and then closed during the Reformation. Sandown Park racecourse now occupies the site. A small section of ruin said to come from the hospital stands at the eastern end of Esher High Street, just outside the racecourse boundary.

Guildford Black Friary, Dominican

This small but very fashionable friary was founded by Queen Eleanor, widow of Henry III, in the 1270s. The friary remained a favourite of royal consorts throughout the rest of the Middle Ages. It closed in 1538. The site is now occupied by the Friary shopping centre.

Guildford Friary of the Sack, Friars of the Sack
One of the genuinely impoverished houses of friars, this establishment had no endowments and the friars carried a sack with which they begged for food and alms. The friary stood on the north side of the town.

Horsley Priory, Benedictine nuns
A small house of which no trace remains.

Laleham Abbey, Benedictine monks
This small house was closed at the Reformation and became the site of a manor house. The house was rebuilt in the nineteenth century and in the 1930s was taken over by the Community of St Peter the Apostle, an Anglo-Catholic order that turned it into a school and a spiritual retreat.

Newark Priory, Augustinian Canons Regular
Dedicated to Our Lady and St Thomas of Canterbury, this house founded by Ruald of Calna and his wife Beatrice in about 1194. It was suppressed in 1538.

Oxenford Priory, Benedictine monks
A small and poor house of monks that stood near Elstead.

Reigate Priory, Augustinian Canons Regular
Founded in about 1230 by the rich and powerful William de Warenne, 6th Earl of Surrey, this house remained prosperous until it was closed in 1536. Priory Park now occupies the site.

Sheen Priory, Carthusian monks
This has the distinction of being the last monastic house to survive in England during the Reformation. It was founded in 1414 by King Henry V adjacent to his palace at Sheen (later renamed Richmond Palace). It was suppressed in 1539 by

Henry VIII, then opened again by his daughter Queen Mary I before being closed again in the 1560s by Queen Elizabeth I.

Sheen Friary, Franciscan Observant Friars

The friary at Sheen was less fortunate than the nearby priory. It was founded in 1499 by King Henry VII as a house for a reformed branch of the Franciscans which had been founded in Siena by St Bernardine in 1400. For some reason, King Henry VIII took against this order and forcibly expelled them from England in 1534, well before the main wave of monastic closures took place.

Syon Priory, Gilbertine Canons Regular and Canonesses

The Gilbertines were the only exclusively English religious order. They were founded in 1131 by St Gilbert of Sempringham, whose first recruits were seven of the pupils at his village school. The Gilbertines wore a black cassock and white hood. They grew to have twenty-six houses, only four of which were of any real size. The Syon Priory was one of the smallest. The English nature of the order did not save them and they were closed down along with the rest by Henry VIII.

Tandridge Priory, Augustinian Canons Regular

Founded in the twelfth century as a hospital and rest home for impoverished clergy, this house was dedicated to St James. It closed in 1535.

Waverley Abbey, Cistercian monks

Waverley was founded in 1128 and dedicated to St Mary. This was the very first Cistercian house in England and opened under the auspices of William Giffard, Bishop of Winchester. It was closed in 1536.

8

LITERARY SURREY

WRITERS WHO HAVE LIVED IN SURREY

Constance Garnett lived at The Cearne, a house in Limpsfield Chart, from 1896 until her death in 1946. Although she wrote several plays, she is best known for her translations into English of Russian works by such masters as Tolstoy, Chekhov, Pushkin and Gogol.

William Congreve lived at the now-demolished Ashley Park just outside Walton-on-Thames from 1717 to 1719. In his youth, Congreve wrote a number of hugely successful comedies for the stage of which *The Way of the World* was probably the most popular. By the time he was living in Surrey, however, he had turned to politics where he was moderately successful. His best known line remains 'Hell hath no fury like a woman scorned'. Or rather, it wasn't, since what he *actually* wrote was 'Heaven has no rage like love to hatred turned, Nor hell a fury like a woman scorned'.

David Garnett lived with his mother Constance Garnett in Limpsfield Chart for many years. In the 1920s he was best known for the novel *Lady into Fox*, for which he won the prestigious James Tate Black Memorial Prize in 1922. Today, however, he is more famous as the author of the novel *Aspects of Love* which in 1989 was turned into a musical by Andrew Lloyd Webber.

Jane Porter, the novelist who wrote *The Scottish Chiefs* in 1810, lived at no. 85 High Street in Esher for a number of years.

This was a fine Georgian townhouse with an impressively large portico adorned with Ionic pillars. It was pulled down in the mid-twentieth century and replaced with a parade of shops. While living in Esher, Porter one day saw a neighbour walk into her study unannounced, then leave again as if in a huff. She later found out that the neighbour had died a few minutes before she saw his figure.

In 1897 the prolific American writer Stephen Crane rented the Ravensbrook House on Snats Hill near Oxted while on a promotional tour of Britain. He wrote a vast number of highly acclaimed novels and short stories, plus some poems that were not so well received. His best known work today is *The Red Badge of Courage*, a novel about the American Civil War that was made into a film starring Audie Murphy in 1951.

In 1865 a mysterious woman calling herself Mrs Mackay and her children came to live at Fern Dell in Mickleham. Among the children was a ten-year-old girl named Mary, of whom nobody took much notice. Although Mrs Mackay kept it a close secret, she was not actually married to Dr Mackay and young Mary and her siblings were illegitimate. At the age of thirty, Mary Mackay published a melodramatic romantic novel entitled *A Romance of Two Worlds* under the name of Marie Corelli. Her works proved to be hugely popular and combined philosophical musings with high drama. As soon as she began earning money, Corelli moved to London and later to Stratford-upon-Avon. Perhaps she did not like Mickleham all that much.

The poet Richard Church lived in a cottage, now a shop, in Limpsfield High Street opposite the Bull Inn for several years from 1916. His best known work is 'Mud', published in 1917. In later years he wrote works for the Labour party and became director of the Oxford Festival of Spoken Poetry.

The idiosyncratic Welsh poet William Davies came to live in a cottage by the churchyard in Limpsfield in 1927. By that time he was a highly regarded poet, but earlier in his life had been a sailor, beggar, farmer, gold miner and tramp. He first wrote poetry in 1905 at the age of thirty-four – he never looked back and went on to fame and fortune.

Anthony Hope lived at Heath Farm in Deans Lane, Walton on the Hill, from 1925 to 1933. Hope wrote a total of thirty-two novels, plus a vast number of short stories. His great fame came in 1894 when he published *The Prisoner of Zenda*, a romantic tale of love, loyalty and betrayal, set in the fictitious east European Kingdom of Ruritania. The book has never been out of print, was made into a play within a year of being published and has been filmed no less than six times.

Richard Brinsley Sheridan was an Irish playwright who achieved fame and fortune in London with a series of popular comedies. In 1796 he bought Polesden Lacey, just outside Great Bookham, to be his country retreat. Writing of his wife he said 'my new house will be a seat of health and happiness where she shall chirp like a bird, bound like a fawn and grow fat as a little pig.' Unfortunately he was mistaken. His beloved Elizabeth and his son Richard both fell dangerously ill with scarlet fever. 'I wish I had never seen the place,' Sheridan wrote as he nursed them. Happily, both survived the illness.

WORKS WRITTEN IN SURREY

The poet and anti-slavery campaigner Anna Barbauld was visiting her brother at his home in Dorking in 1796 when the lovely countryside inspired her to write a series of nature poems quite unlike her usual style of work. The most widely read of these was 'Burford Bridge', a work about the eponymous bridge over the Mole, now replaced by a rather soulless modern affair carrying the A24.

These days Benjamin Disraeli is best known as the Prime Minister of Britain from 1874 to 1880, but back in the 1840s his fame was as a novelist. His political novel *Coningsby* was planned and partly written while he was staying with his friend Henry Hope at Deepdene, a now-demolished mansion that stood on the eastern edge of Dorking.

Despite its title, *The Hungarian Brothers* was written at no. 85 High Street, Esher. The author, Anna Maria Porter was a very successful Scottish novelist who moved from Scotland to Esher as soon as her books started selling in large numbers.

Jane Austen's novel *Emma* was begun while the novelist was staying with her married cousin Cassandra Cooke in Great Bookham. Jane Austen was a frequent visitor to Great Bookham, staying with Cassandra on more than one occasion for some weeks at a time.

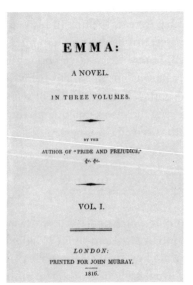

The frontispiece to the first edition of Jane Austen's novel Emma. *The work was begun in Surrey and several Surrey places are featured in the text.*

Another writer who moved to Esher as soon as he enjoyed financial success was William Howitt who moved to West End Cottage, between Esher and West End, within months of his work *The Book of the Seasons* achieving high sales. Unlike Porter, however, he did not care for the place. He stayed only three years before moving to Heidelberg in Germany. Howitt must have missed Surrey, though, for in 1866 he came back to England and moved into The Orchard, a grand house at the corner of Rayleigh Drive and Hare Lane between Esher and Claygate.

D.H. Lawrence wrote his poem 'Whether or Not' when staying with fellow writer Constance Garnett in Limpsfield Chart.

One of the best-selling authors of the sixteenth century lived in Reigate Castle from 1547 to 1553. John Foxe worked in Reigate as tutor to the children of Henry, Earl of Surrey, but his fame comes from the book widely known as *Foxe's Book of Martyrs*, though its official title was *Actes and Monuments of these Latter and Perillous Days, Touching Matters of the Church*.

An illustration from Foxe's Book of Martyrs. *The book included many religious essays and tracts but became best known for its section on Protestant martyrs executed by the Catholics.*

The vast book was published in 1563 and covered a wide range of theological and historical matter, but its most sensational and popular section was that concerning the martyrdoms of Protestants at the hands of Catholics. Perhaps not surprisingly, Foxe spent much of his life on the run from vengeful Catholic authorities. It is thought that he did some of the writing of his book while living in Reigate.

In 1818 John Keats was under enormous pressure from his publisher to produce something that could be printed for sale, following some months of inactivity while he nursed his sick brother. Keats decided to get away from family and friends to concentrate on work, so he took a room at the Fox and Hounds north of Dorking (it has now been expanded and renamed the Burford Bridge Hotel). Locked up for weeks on end, Keats produced the epic poem 'Endymion', which runs to 4,000 lines. The poem began 'A thing of beauty is a joy for ever', and although it is now regarded as a classic, it did not do very well at the time.

Another writer who took rooms at the Fox and Hounds (Burford Bridge Hotel) to get a work finished was Robert Louis Stevenson who came here in 1882 to wrap up *The New Arabian Nights*. Unlike Keats's effort, Stevenson's sold well.

A Passage to India was a novel published in 1924 by E.M. Forster. He had gathered the background material for the book during his own voyage to India some years earlier, but the book was written at the writer's home in Abinger Hammer. The book won the James Tait Black Memorial Prize in 1924 and was included in *Time* magazine's list of 100 great novels of the twentieth century. In 1984 the book was filmed by David Lean.

The year after *A Passage to India* hit the big screen a second E.M. Forster book written in Surrey was also made into a film, this time starring Helena Bonham Carter and Judi Dench. *A Room with a View* was written at Abinger Hammer and published in 1908. The story is a romance following the adventures of a pretty young English girl named Lucy Honeychurch in Florence and England.

The Paying Guest is not one of George Gissing's best novels, and it sold hardly any copies at all when it appeared in 1895. Gissing had written it while living at no. 7 Clifton Terrace, Dorking. The failure came as a blow after the success of his earlier novels such as *The Nether World* of 1889. Perhaps as a result he moved away from Dorking – and almost immediately returned to form and financial success.

George Meredith's novel *Diana of the Crossways* is an account of an intelligent and forceful woman trapped in a miserable marriage. It was widely rumoured to be based on Meredith's friendship with society beauty and author Caroline Norton. Quite what Mrs Meredith made of the book and its success is not recorded. The book was written in the little chalet-style study on the slopes of Box Hill overlooking Dorking, where Meredith had his family home. Meredith – and his wife – are buried in Dorking.

The poet Algernon Charles Swinburne was out for a walk on Esher Common in 1862 when he sat down to rest on the Round Hill, a beauty spot now almost obliterated by the junction of the A3 and A244. Suddenly inspired, he whipped out his notebook and began composing his famous poem 'Laus Veneris'. Swinburne had a reputation for loose living, but was later to be dismissed by Oscar Wilde (no sluggard when it came to loose living) with the words, 'Swinburne is a braggart in matters of vice, who had done everything he could to convince his fellow citizens of his homosexuality and bestiality without being in the slightest degree a homosexual or a bestializer.'

It is sometimes said that the British tradition of stage farces was created by John Maddison Morton. And undoubtedly his most popular farce was *Box and Cox* which was written in Laburnum Cottage in Bridge Road, Chertsey, in 1847. The play was astonishingly popular and was staged by companies up and down the kingdom, earning Morton an amazing £7,000 in royalties. He went on to write a string of other popular farces such as *Going to the Derby* (1848), *Slasher and Crasher!* (1848), *Your Life's in Danger* (1848), *Where There's a Will There's a Way* (1849), *My Precious Betsy* (1850), *Sent to the Tower* (1850), *Grimshaw, Bagshaw, and Bradshaw* (1851), *The Woman I Adore!* (1852), *A Capital Match!* (1852), *Waiting for an Omnibus in the Lowther Arcade on a Rainy Day* (1854), *A Game of Romps* (1855),

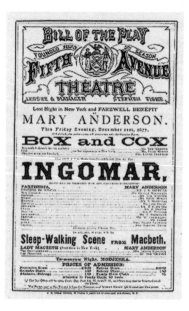

How Stout You're Getting! (1855), *The Rights and Wrongs of Women* (1856), *The Little Savage* (1858), *Wooing One's Wife* (1861), *Drawing Rooms, Second Floor, and Attics* (1864), *My Wife's Bonnet* (1865) and *A Day's Fishing* (1869). He was nothing if not prolific.

A poster for a play written John Maddison Morton, who was born in Chertsey but later found worldwide fame.

Thomas Day was born in London in 1748. At an early age he inherited a fortune, then got another by marrying a rich heiress. Contrary to most such men, Day kept hold of his money with great care. He bought Anningsley Park near Ottershaw and settled down to living within his means while churning out a vast amount of humourless and depressing works about how awful life was for anyone who was poor or who had to work for a living. He died in 1789 and, unsurprisingly, hardly anyone bothers to read his works these days.

AND ONE THAT WASN'T

In 1808 the great playwright Richard Brinsley Sheridan rented Randall's Farm, now a cemetery just outside Leatherhead, for fifteen months. He did not produce a single word the whole time he was there. Apparently the fishing in the River Mole was so good he could not concentrate on anything else.

FICTIONAL CHARACTERS BASED ON REAL SURREY PEOPLE

In 1875 George Meredith published his favourite novel *Beauchamp's Career* in which he follows the career of a naval officer turned radical politician named Nevil Beauchamp. In the course of the novel Meredith pokes fun at the navy, radical aristocrats and the British Establishment. The lead character of Nevil Beauchamp was based on the real life retired officer Captain Maxse who lived in Esher during the 1840s and 1850s and was a personal friend of Meredith.

He obviously enjoyed basing his fictional characters on real ones. Sir Alexander Duff-Gordon, a baronet, served as the basis for Jocelyn in the novel *Evan Harrington*, published in 1861.

Meredith went for a hat-trick of Surrey personages in his books when he came across an encampment of gypsies on Esher Common. He at once put them in fictionalised form into his latest work *The English Roadside*.

WRITERS WHO WERE BORN IN SURREY

Florence Charlesworth (better known under her married name of Florence Barclay) was born in the vicarage of Limpsfield in 1862. She wrote eleven books, several of which were made into silent movies. Her best known work is the 1909 novel *The Rosary*, a lengthy work telling of a romantic love battling against the odds. It was republished in 2002.

The diarist John Evelyn was born at Wotton House, near Wotton, on 31 October 1620. He said of the house, 'It was sweetly environed with those delicious streames and venerable woods, as in the judgment of strangers, as well as Englishmen, it may be compared to one of the most tempting and pleasant seates in the nation.' In his lifetime Evelyn was perhaps best known for his works on botany and gardening, though it is his diary that has ensured his lasting fame.

Albert Smith was born in a house beside Chertsey church in 1816. He later wrote a string of comedy novels and plays which earned him a comfortable lifestyle. He first found fame, however, performing what we would today call a one-man show, which was composed of himself telling humorous anecdotes about his journey to Constantinople and back.

WRITERS WHO DIED IN SURREY

William Harrison Ainsworth died in his Belvedere House in St Mary's Road, Reigate, on 3 January 1882. Ainsworth wrote thirty-nine novels, of which the most famous is *Rookwood*, published in 1834. The book is a strange blend of Gothic horror and historical realism, and features the highwayman Dick Turpin as one of its principal characters. Several of his books were made into stage plays and he also contributed to popular magazines. After 1860 Ainsworth did little work and by the time of his death he was almost forgotten outside of Surrey.

Joseph Spence must be counted rather unlucky. During his lifetime he was hailed as a great poet and historian, producing a number of hugely successful works. With the proceeds he bought a house in Byfleet which had extensive grounds stretching north-east over St George's Hill. There he lived out an idyllic life in semi-retirement. On 20 August 1768 he went out for a walk, tripped and fell into the pond on St George's Hill. He drowned before he could be dragged out.

The seventeenth-century poet Abraham Cowley had an adventurous life. He fought for the king in the Civil War, and spent more than twelve years in exile as a result. He was close to Charles II in exile and carried out a number of diplomatic and spy missions for the would-be king. When Charles returned to his throne in 1660, Cowley came with him but, now beginning to feel his age, Cowley chose to retire from public life. He was given a small estate near Chertsey by the Duke of Buckingham by way of thanks for his work for the king. He was also given a house in Guildford Street, Chertsey, where he spent the rest of his life. He died here in 1667 and was buried in Westminster Abbey. His love poems were generally reckoned to be the finest work in the English language in the mid-seventeenth century.

The name of Katherine Bradley is not terribly well known, which is because she wrote under the name of Michael Field. Bradley/Field moved to live in Reigate in 1888 and died there in 1914. As Field she wrote several plays and much poetry, including some passionate, decidedly racy love poems, and contributed prolifically to magazines and periodicals. She caused a scandal with a love affair with another woman and her continuing friendship with Oscar Wilde after his disgrace.

In 1888 Matthew Arnold died at his house, Pain's Hill Cottage in Cobham. The cottage has since been demolished and a cul-de-sac named Matthew Arnold Close built on the spot. Arnold was famous as both a poet and a school inspector, though he was largely retired by the time he came to live in Cobham. He did, however, write the poem 'Matthias' while living here as a tribute to his recently deceased pet canary.

The prolific and tempestuous Irish writer William Maginn died of tuberculosis in Walton-on-Thames in 1842 and is buried in the churchyard. In the course of his career, Maginn wrote learned works on Shakespeare, collaborated with Dickens, authored scandalously pornographic stories (under an assumed name) and drank or gambled away his vast earnings. He also fought one of the last duels in England when he exchanged pistol shots with Grantley Berkeley MP as a result of a quarrel over a review Maginn had written of a novel by Berkeley.

Dorothy Osborne, Lady Temple, was visiting Moor Park at Farnham in 1695 when she was taken ill and died. She is buried in Westminster Abbey. Osborne is best known for her collected letters, which show a lady of wit and charm. Earlier in her life she had visited Epsom often to take the waters.

WRITERS WHO MARRIED IN SURREY

Fanny Burney was already an established novelist and playwright when in 1793 she came to visit her friend Susannah Lock at Norbury Park near Mickleham. Staying just on the other side of the Mole at Juniper Hall was a group of French noblemen who had fled to England to escape the guillotine.

One of these was General Alexandre D'Arblay, with whom Fanny soon fell in love. The Burney family disapproved of the Frenchman on the grounds that he was French, Catholic and penniless. However, Fanny was financially independent due to the success of her writings, so she went ahead and married her Frenchman anyway. They bought a house at nearby West Humble that they named Camilla Cottage after Fanny's most profitable novel. The two lived happily in England and France until the general died in 1818.

WORKS WRITTEN ABOUT SURREY

Poet John Skelton obviously liked a decent pint of beer. In 1499 he was appointed to be tutor to young Prince Henry (later King Henry VIII) at Nonsuch Manor. At every possible opportunity, however, he slipped off to the Running Horse Inn, still standing in Bridge Road, Leatherhead.

One of his best loved poems, a long raucous tale called 'The Tunning of Elynour Rummyng' is set at the Running Horse. The poem opens

> And this comely dame,
> I understande, her name
> Is Elynour Rummynge,
> At home in her wonnynge;
> And as men say

> She dwelt in Sothray,
> In a certayne stede
> Bysyde Lederhede.
> She is a tonnysh gyb;
> The devyll and she be syb.
> But to make up my tale,
> She breweth noppy ale,
> And maketh therof port sale
> To travellars, to tynkers,
> To sweters, to swynkers,
> And all good ale drynkers,
> That wyll nothynge spare,
> But drynke tyll they stare,
> And brynge themselfe bare,
> With, Now away the mare,
> And let us slay care,
> As wyse as an hare!

Oh well, it was popular 500 years ago.

In 1673 Thomas Shadwell wrote and staged the immensely successful comedy *Epsom Wells* based on his experiences of visiting Epsom to take the waters. The play is a bawdy and cleverly plotted comedy that mixes farce with witty social commentary. Shadwell went on to become Poet Laureate in 1689.

Celia Fiennes was the daughter of a Roundhead colonel who, in 1684, inherited a considerable fortune. She spent the next twenty years travelling around Britain and produced *Through England on a Side Saddle* as a memoir written up from the notes she made as she travelled. She did not care much for Surrey. 'Unpaved', 'dirty' and 'dank' were some of the words she used. She was particularly dismissive of the medicinal well at Epsom saying it was 'a dirty old wooden building, very dark.'

Abinger Harvest was a collection of short stories written by E.M. Forster while he was living at Abinger Hammer. Although some of the tales were obviously based on real events and characters around the village, Forster carefully disguised them.

The novel *Emma* by Jane Austen features a picnic that takes place on Box Hill. It is often said that the main village in the novel is based on Cobham, though Austen never stated this clearly.

In 1836 Charles Dickens visited Chertsey to see the house once lived in by Abraham Cowley. He stayed in the Black Swan, which later featured in *Oliver Twist*, and met a man (whom he never publicly identified) who found fictional fame as Mr Pecksniff in *Martin Chuzzlewit*.

The play *Blanche Heriot* was written by Albert Smith in 1842 and subtitled *The Chertsey Curfew*. It retells a local legend set during the Wars of the Roses in the 1470s. Blanche is a local lass who is in love with a dashing young soldier named Neville Audley. This Audley is loyal to the Lancastrian cause in the wars, but is captured by Yorkist soldiers and is sentenced to be executed when the curfew bell sounds the next day. Blanche, however, knows that a pardon is on its way from London and locks herself in the bell tower of Chertsey Abbey in order to stop the curfew bell from being rung. A succession of adventures follow, but all ends happily with the pardon arriving before the bell is rung. The old curfew bell of Chertsey Abbey was cast in 1310 and is now hung in the parish church.

Born sometime about 1705 – nobody is quite sure when – Stephen Duck became a vicar who wrote popular poetry to get religious and moral ideas across to lay people. His works were immensely popular in their day, though they are rarely read today. In 1752 Duck became vicar at Byfleet. One of his works was about the local countryside. Entitled 'Caesar's Camp' it concerned the earthworks on St George's Hill. At the time the fort was thought to be a Roman work, though it is now known to date to the Celtic Iron Age about 200 years before the Romans came this way.

Newark Priory is a ruined priory near Pyrford. In 1807 the poet Thomas Love Peacock was visiting the ruins when he chanced to meet a local young lady named Fanny Faulkner. A romance blossomed, but then went wrong and Fanny married somebody else. Peacock was heartbroken and wrote a whole string of poems about Newark Priory. Even his marriage in 1820 to the noted beauty Jane Griffith did not stop his outpourings as the final poem about Newark Priory – entitled 'Revisiting Newark Priory' –was written in 1842. Quite what Jane made of her husband's devotion to a lost love is not recorded.

The great science fiction novel *The War of the Worlds* by H.G. Wells opens in Ottershaw at an observatory from where explosions are sighted on the surface of Mars. The action then moves to Horsell Common where what seems to be a meteor crashes to earth. From the meteor emerge Martians who proceed to put together a fighting machine armed with a heat ray. Other Martians land elsewhere on Earth and the action in the book then moves away from Surrey to follow the course of the invasion and the human resistance. A fine statue of a Martian fighting machine now dominates the centre of Woking.

9

NATURAL SURREY

AREAS OF WOODLAND
OPEN TO THE PUBLIC IN SURREY

Banstead Woods
Lying just outside Banstead, these woods have a car park located near the junction of the B2032 and B2219. The woods cover a large area and are easily accessed by a network of footpaths. Adjacent to the woods on the south lies the Fames Rough, an area of rough grassland.

Chantries
Owned by Guildford Council, the Chantries stretch from the edge of the town south to St Martha's Church. The mixed woodland includes some stands of huge, ancient oaks as well as managed coppice and more open areas. There are numerous, well-used footpaths.

Devil's Punchbowl
This well-known beauty spot occupies a huge hollow in the downs just outside Hindhead. The marked nature trails through the Devil's Punchbowl start at the car park and lead out on to nearby heathland as well as weaving through the woodlands of the Punchbowl itself.

Hurtwood
The 4,000 acres of Hurtwood cover not only Hurt Wood itself, but also Holmbury Hill, Pitch Hill and Smithwood Common. Most of the land is covered by commercial stands of pine, but

there are some stretches of wild woodland as well. There are twelve car parks and a network of paths.

Leith Hill
Most of the woodlands on and around Leith Hill are now owned by the National Trust and are open to the public. The hill itself is 965ft tall, the highest point in south-eastern England, and is topped by a tower that is open to the public.

Limpsfield Common
Owned by the National Trust and others, this extensive area of beech and conifer woodlands is interspersed with heathland. There are several parking areas and picnic grounds.

Ranmore Common
There are over 500 acres of forest owned by the National Trust here, but another 250 acres in private ownership is open to the public. The forest occupies a patch of wet clay soil that overlies the chalk downs here.

Staffhurst Wood
Running along the border with Kent, this oak woodland also includes sycamore, birch and maple. It is managed by the county council as a nature reserve.

10 WILD PLANTS IN SURREY YOU MUST NOT TOUCH

Death cap – fungus
Black bryony – herbaceous climber
Deadly nightshade – branching herbaceous bush
Cuckoo pint – perennial tuber
Destroying angel – fungus

Yew – tree
Henbane – part of the potato family
Water dropwort – part of the parsley family
Devil's boletus – fungus
Panther cap – fungus

10 WILD PLANTS IN SURREY YOU CAN EAT

Blackberry
Dandelion leaves
Fat hen
Field mushroom
Stinging nettle (use gloves when gathering)
Wild garlic
Lesser celandine
Cow parsley
Ox-eye daisy
Chickweed

WOODLAND BIRDS FOUND IN SURREY

Goldcrest

Britain's smallest bird with a length of just 3.5in, the Goldcrest is famed for its aggressive nature. As a small bird it is vulnerable to cold winters, so it lays two clutches of 7 to 10 eggs each summer to keep numbers up. The nest is usually built in a conifer tree, hanging from a branch as a clump of moss and grass – in Surrey the Goldcrest often adds wool taken from downland bushes where it has snagged from grazing sheep. It generally feeds on insects, especially flies.

Blue Tit

Perhaps the best loved of Surrey's birds is the Blue Tit, famous for its acrobatics on garden bird feeders. The distinctive blue, white and yellow markings make this easily recognisable. In the days when milkmen left bottles of milk on most doorsteps, the Blue Tit learned how to peck through the foil lids to get at the milk within. One morning in 1967 the caretaker at Merstham Primary School counted that 57 out of 300 milk bottles had been opened by Blue Tits in the half hour between the milkman leaving them and his going out to collect them. More recently, Blue Tits have developed a habit of tearing strips from paper that they find in recycling boxes. In winter Blue Tits will form large flocks that race through the woodlands stirring up insects, that are quickly snapped up.

Great Tit

As its name suggests, the Great Tit is the largest of the tit family. Gardeners in Surrey often put up nesting boxes for Great Tits due to the fact that these birds feed their young on caterpillars – a typical nesting pair will get through about 7,000 caterpillars while raising a brood. The bird has a wide vocabulary that ranges from a 'teacher' to a 'pink' to a sound a bit like a saw in use.

Robin

In 1961 the International Council for Bird Preservation chose the Robin as the national bird of Britain due to the fact that in Britain the Robin ventures close to humans, but avoids them elsewhere across its range. Robins adorn Christmas cards due to the fact that they do not migrate south, instead prancing about in gardens searching for food among the frost and snows. Come February the cock Robins begin to sing loudly from fence posts and prominent branches. Unseen, the females are skulking about nearby looking for a mate.

Chiffchaff

Often mistaken for the very similar Willow Warbler, the Chiffchaff can be distinguished by its call, which, unsurprisingly, sounds like 'chiff-chaff'. The bird arrives early in spring, usually the middle of March, when it will take up a position on a fencepost or tree branch to sing loudly and so claim a territory. The birds nest in a dense bush and raise a single brood. The Chiffchaff stays late as well as arriving early, not leaving Surrey until late October.

Blackcap

Named for the glossy black top to the head sported by the male, the Blackcap is heard more often than it is seen. The fluid, warbling song of this bird pours forth from dense cover, but will change to a harsh 'tau-tau' call if a human gets close enough to alarm the bird. They arrive in Surrey during April and stay until September before heading south for the winter.

Wood Warbler

This charming bird is in Surrey only from April to August, and even then it frequents dense and well-established woodland so it rarely ventures into gardens. In Surrey it prefers beechwoods that are often seen on the downs. It is usually glimpsed only when the male carries out its courtship display flight, when it will dart about in woodlands quivering its wings rapidly.

Great Green Woodpecker

Although primarily a woodland bird, this woodpecker may venture on to garden lawns in search of insects. They may also be seen taking fruit from trees. When courting, the birds may chase each other around trees or display to each other with spread tails and drooping wings.

The one that isn't – the Wryneck

Back in the 1930s the Wryneck was a common sight in Surrey woodlands. Since then it has declined rapidly. The last nesting pair was spotted in the 1960s and now years on end pass without one being seen at all. This bird is a member of the woodpecker family, but it feeds by gathering insects from the ground or on trees without pecking holes.

Coal Tit

This bird can be recognised by the white spot on the nape of its neck. This is the shyest of Surrey's tits and is seen only rarely on bird feeders, though it will venture into gardens with plenty of dense shrubs. They generally prefer coniferous woodlands, where they nest in holes or hollows of trees. The female sits on the eggs, while the male feeds her. If a human or other potential danger approaches the nest too closely the female will issue an odd, snake-like hissing noise.

Nightingale

Not exactly common in Surrey, this shy bird is best known for its fantastic song. The males arrive from Africa in April and at once seek to establish territories in woodland or on heaths by perching on a prominent branch and pouring forth the melodic song for minutes at a time. They go back to Africa by late August.

WETLANDS OPEN TO THE PUBLIC IN SURREY

Basingstoke Canal

This canal was completed in 1794 to run from the Wey at Byfleet through Woking to Basingstoke. It was last used for commercial purposes in the First World War and then lay derelict until the 1990s when it was restored. The towpath makes for a lovely country walk in the course of which waterbirds and wetland plants can be spotted.

Thursley Common

Lying amid an extensive sandy heath, the bogs of Thursley are home to a huge variety of insects and rare wetland plants. It has been recognised as being a site of scientific interest of national importance and access may be restricted at certain times of year.

HEATHLANDS OPEN TO THE PUBLIC IN SURREY

Blackheath

Spreading from Shamley Green to Chilworth, Blackheath is an extensive area of birch and pine woodland growing on a grey sand soil that is too poor for farming and too unstable for buildings. The stands of trees are separated by wide stretches of heather and gorse.

Chobham Common

Covering 1,445 acres, Chobham Common is now cut by the M3, but is otherwise little changed from its natural state. The land is made up of infertile sand on which little will grow other than heather, gorse and birch. There are ten car parks, linked by a wide ranging network of footpaths and bridleways. The common is the supposed location of the famous Chobham Treacle Mine.

Crooksbury Hill

Lying beside Elstead, these 204 acres of heathland have stands of chestnut trees where local schoolchildren have traditionally collected conkers in the autumn.

Frensham Common

Spreading south of Frensham, this extensive area of heath is covered by heather and birch. It is best known for Frensham Great Pond, which covers over 100 acres. It was created in the 1270s by monks from Winchester who used it to raise fish for the table. The pond is now a noted watersports centre and a focus for anglers.

Headley Heath

An unusual patch of sandy heath perched on the downs, Headley Heath is mostly covered by bracken and heather. Roe deer like to hide up in the bracken during the day.

Puttenham Common

There are 470 acres of public open space here that are mostly covered by sandy heath, with some stands of alder and birch. There are three car parks and numerous paths.

HEATHLAND BIRDS FOUND IN SURREY

Nightjar

The Nightjar spends the day hiding among woodland before venturing out at dusk to feast on flying insects that it catches over open fields and pastures. When night falls it returns to a roost and gives the 'churrr' call that gives it its name. It nests on the ground in woodland, where fallen leaves and bark make the brooding bird almost impossible to see. It is in Surrey only for the summer, returning to the African grasslands in the winter.

Yellowhammer

This shy bird almost never ventures into gardens, even large ones, and stays as far away from people as it can. Despite this it can be numerous across Surrey heaths where its call of 'little-bit-of-bread-and-no-cheeeeeeese' is a common sound from March to November. In cold winters, Yellowhammers from Eastern Europe move west and so the populations of this bird in Surrey may actually grow in January and February.

Tree Pipit

The archetypal LBJ (Little Brown Job), the Tree Pipit is dull brown in plumage and easily missed. However, the male has a truly spectacular courtship display. Starting from a perch on a bush or low tree, the bird will take flight while singing and climb steeply up into the sky. Long after it vanishes from sight, the bird can still be heard as its voice builds to a crescendo. Once it stops climbing, the bird continues to sing more sedately as it spirals down to alight on the same perch from where it began.

Dartford Warbler

Surrey is about as far east as this pretty little bird gets. It ceased being seen around Dartford almost a century ago. This little bird is horribly vulnerable to cold winters. In 1963 it was down to about ten pairs and suffered again in the winter of 2009/10. Fortunately it breeds prolifically and usually recovers its numbers within a couple of years.

GRASSLANDS OPEN TO THE PUBLIC IN SURREY

Bookham Common

Strictly speaking this area covers three commons: Great Bookham Common, Little Bookham Common and Banks Common, but they all run into each other and the 447 acres can be explored together easily. The commons lie on heavy clay soil and so can be waterlogged at times, which can make walking sticky going. Most of the ground is covered by grassland, but there are stretches of oak woodland and thickets of blackthorn or hawthorn.

Epsom Common

Stretching west from Epsom to embrace Ashtead Common and Stoke Wood, this area of open grasslands and sometimes dense stands of timber extends across to Oxshott. There are two ponds that once belonged to Chertsey Abbey, where fish were raised for the monastic table, but that are now local angling haunts.

GRASSLAND BIRDS FOUND IN SURREY

Tawny Owl

This is by far the most numerous owl in Surrey and is the one responsible for the familiar 'tu-whit tu-whoo' call. It usually nests in a hole in a tree, but on the sandier soils may take over a rabbit burrow. During daylight hours it usually roosts in a tree where a branch leaves the main trunk and is difficult to spot. It feeds on small rodents, beetles and any other small animal it manages to overpower.

Woodcock

This bird prefers broadleaved woods that have plenty of open glades or rides where it can feed. It nests on the ground and if disturbed the adult may carry the young off in its feet or between its thighs. Beautifully camouflaged, the Woodcock is generally difficult to see, but from March to July the male will at dawn and dusk fly around its territory making a high-pitched call and flying in a twisting pattern that makes it easy to spot.

Partridge

Although it was a native bird, the Partridge has been so interbred with game birds brought from Eastern Europe that the birds found today in Surrey are a very mixed bunch. The birds prefer to nest on grasslands close to woods or dense thickets of shrubs.

WILD MAMMALS FOUND IN SURREY

Grey Squirrel

This rodent was introduced from North America in the 1870s and rapidly took over woodland in Surrey from the native Red Squirrel. It is about 10in long, plus an 8in tail, and has a dense grey-brown fur which is longer and paler in winter than in summer. In wild woodland there are usually around five per acre, but the population can be higher in gardens.

Fox

Traditionally an animal of the Surrey countryside, the fox has been invading gardens since the 1950s and by the 1980s was established in town centres as well. In rural areas it feeds on rabbits, mice, voles, frogs, birds and squirrels, but in urban areas will raid bins and feast on human litter. Apart from the breeding season, roughly March to July, the fox is a solitary animal which guards its territory vigorously.

Rabbit

The rabbit was introduced from France in the twelfth century during the warm climatic conditions known as the Medieval Warm Period. It went into decline and almost vanished during the Little Ice Age of the seventeenth and eighteenth centuries, but as the climate began to warm again after about 1800, rabbit numbers boomed as they bred like, well, rabbits. Myxomatosis slashed numbers in the 1950s, but the rabbit population has grown again. The rabbits emerge to feed at dawn and dusk, with each individual eating about a pound of greenery each day. Rabbits can be hugely destructive on farmland.

Roe Deer

This is the only deer native to Surrey. It prefers woodland and is so shy that few Surrey residents are aware of just how many of these animals there are in the county. Each Roe stands about 2ft tall and the male alone have antlers. They live in small family groups consisting of a doe, buck and their offspring.

Weasel

The smallest hunting mammal in Surrey, the weasel can grow to be a foot long and is covered in an attractive chestnut fur on top with white beneath. It hunts frogs, mice and voles at night, but will come out in the daytime if it is hungry. Weasels have been known to raid chicken runs for eggs and chicks, but will tackle an adult bird only rarely.

Stoat

In summer a stoat could be mistaken for a weasel were it not for the fact that it is about twice as large. In winter, however, the stoat adopts a whitish coat and black tail that once made it highly valued as a fur animal. Stoat numbers declined badly when Myxomatosis hit rabbits, but are now improving again.

Wild Boar

The Wild Boar became extinct across Britain in late medieval times. After the Second World War a few began to be farmed and a handful escaped into the wild. It was the savage storm of 1987 that led to a mass of escapees as fences were torn down by falling trees and large numbers of farmed boar escaped. By 1989 a breeding population of around 50 was established in woodland along the Kent/Sussex border. This population has now grown to around 300 individuals and they have been sighted moving into woodland in southern Surrey. Boar prefer woodland and are generally shy animals, though they can be dangerous if cornered. The males usually live alone, though females and young live in groups of a dozen or more. They are active only around dawn and dusk.

Common Shrew

Common in Surrey woodland, this 3in-long mammal hunts insects, worms and other small creatures that it consumes with a voracious appetite. It does not hibernate, but continues to seek food throughout the winter.

Pygmy Shrew

Less numerous than the Common Shrew, the Pygmy Shrew is only about half the size of its larger cousin and prefers Surrey's open lands and grasslands. Like the Common Shrew it is a dark grey-brown above and a dirty white below.

WILD REPTILES FOUND IN SURREY

Grass Snake

Although it is most often seen when basking in meadows, hence its name, the Grass Snake hunts in and round water where it seeks fish, frogs, eggs and young birds. It is a dark green above, pale green below and has vertical black bars along its side.

Adder

This is the most common snake in Surrey, and the only venomous one. Adders are easily recognised by the zigzag pattern of brown and yellow along the back. They prefer grassland and heaths, being seen only if they are basking in the sun and cannot be bothered to move. The rest of the time they prowl the undergrowth hunting rodents, birds and insects. They hibernate in burrows from December to March.

Common Lizard

This hardy animal may grow to be 6in long and is dark brown, with paler spots along its back. It hunts insects, spiders and other small animals across the heaths and woods where it lives.

Unlike most reptiles that lay eggs, the Common Lizard gives birth to live young. This helps it to survive in cooler regions of the world as eggs are vulnerable to chilly weather.

Slow Worm

Despite its name, this creature is actually a lizard that has evolved not to have legs. It burrows in leaf mould and loose soil in woodland or beside hedgerows where it hunts for earthworms and other invertebrates.

DOWNLAND OPEN TO THE PUBLIC IN SURREY

Box Hill

The National Trust owns about 1,000 acres of grass and forest on Box Hill which is open free of charge to the public, though there is a charge for using the car park. There is also a café and a shop, where leaflets giving the routes of recommended walks can be found. The most popular features of Box Hill are the views looking south over the Weald to the South Downs in the far distance. They are stunning.

Hawkhurst

This nature reserve lies just outside Gomshall and is jointly owned by the National Trust and Surrey County Council. It is carefully managed to keep it under grass and juniper, with invasive hawthorn being regularly cleared.

Newlands Corner

With a large car park, café and picnic area, Newlands Corner is hugely popular with those coming out of Guildford for a country walk. Most of the publicly accessible area is downland grass, but there are also stretches of forest.

10

THE RIVERS

Abbey River

Named for the mighty Chertsey Abbey that formerly stood on its banks, the Abbey River is really an old course of the Thames that still carries some water from that much larger river. The Abbey leaves the Thames at Penton Hook, heading south to Chertsey. At Chertsey it turns east and then falls back into the Thames by Chertsey Bridge.

Beam Brook

This is the first large stream to enter the Mole. It rises in woodland south-east of Capel and heads north-east through Cudworth. As it flows the Beam picks up water from various smaller streams before it empties into the Mole by the sewage works north-west of Horley.

River Ember

The River Ember is, strictly speaking, part of the River Mole. The Mole splits in two just north of Lower Green near Esher, and joins together again at East Molesey just before entering the Thames. The southern branch is known as the River Ember, while the northern branch remains the River Mole. The marshy island between the two is now occupied by the Island Barn Reservoir. Originally the Ember and the Mole entered the Thames separately close to Creek Road, but when the Hampton Court Way was constructed in the 1930s the Mole was diverted to flow into the Ember. In 1968 there were extensive floods around the Ember that caused large amounts of damage. Subsequent engineering works to prevent future flooding involved cutting off a bend in the Ember near Orchard Lane and the construction of an entirely new riverbed to the west. The aptly named Summer Road crossed the Ember by way of a ford until these anti-flood works were carried out. The ford was blocked off and the road is now a cul-de-sac.

Gad Brook

The Gad rises on Holmwood Common, then heads east past Brockham Park to join the Mole south of Betchworth.

River Mole

The River Mole rises at Baldhorns Copse, just south of the Sussex border, then meanders on a twisting 50-mile course through Surrey to enter the Thames at Molesey. The first notable landmark along the route is Gatwick airport, which was in Surrey until boundary changes moved it to Sussex in the 1970s. The Mole then passes Horley and Sidlow before leaving Reigate a few miles to the north and moving on to pass Brockham and flow through Dorking. Just north of Dorking the Mole heads directly for the towering North Downs. The river has cut itself a chasm in the hills that is known as the Mole Gap. This has long been an important route for humans and animals through the downs, with both the railway and a dual carriageway running alongside the river. The underlying rock here is chalk, which is both permeable to water and easily eroded. There are a series of swallow holes along the mole here, down which large amounts of water vanish to flow through underground passages. In very dry summers the Mole can dry up on the surface along this stretch. At Leatherhead the Mole emerges from its steep-sided valley on to more open clay soils once again. All the water that left the river in the chalk rejoins it through springs and upwelling streams. The Mole then flows through central Leatherhead before heading north-west to Stoke D'Abernon. At Cobham it follows a long meander to the west before sweeping back and heading north-east to flow between Esher and Hersham and so to Molesey and the Thames.

Because most of the upper reaches and many of the tributaries drain water from relatively impermeable clay, the Mole has long been prone to flooding as heavy rainfall runs off the clays and straight into the river. The floods of 1968 were especially destructive and led to a range of anti-flood measures such as embankments, dredging and even the digging of new courses in places.

After the Second World War, the Mole became heavily polluted due to factories and other developments taking place along its banks. However, since 1990 determined efforts have been made to improve the water quality and it is now one of the cleanest rivers in southern England. The Common Frog is numerous along the river, as are two species introduced from Europe – the Marsh Frog and the Edible Frog. The Smooth Newt is another amphibian which appears in large numbers in the Mole. Perhaps because of its diverse geology, the Mole has an unusually wide range of fish species. These include brown trout, brook lamprey, eel, chub, dace, roach, barbel, pike and bleak. Botanists have found that the greater dodder, a rare parasitic plant, is common along the Mole.

River Ock

This rises at Hambledon, then flows north past Enton, Witley and Milford to Ockford. It enters the Wey at Godalming.

River Rye

The River Rye rises on Ashtead Common, drawing water from a series of springs west of the Wells Estate. The salty waters from the original Epsom Salts Spring originally flowed into the Rye. After passing north of Ashtead itself, the river passes under the M25 and A243 before emerging on to the outskirts of Leatherhead at Bridge Close. It then passes through an industrial estate to flow past Teazel Wood and over open ground to enter the Mole near to the Fetcham Park United football ground. During the Second World War the lower courses of the river were straightened and dredged out to improve the drainage of the riverside meadows so that they could be turned over to arable use. Since the 1990s the river has been returning to a more natural condition and the meadows are again being used for grazing.

The Rythe

This stream rises on the wooded western slopes of Telegraph Hill near Claygate. It then flows north past Loseberry Farm east of Claygate and across Littleworth Common to reach Thames Ditton. The Rythe is heavily embanked here to prevent flooding and passes between suburban gardens to go under the old Portsmouth Road at Winter's Bridge before entering the Thames beside Ferry Road.

Tanners Brook

Tanners Brook rises near North Holmwood then runs north through Bushbury to join the Mole near Brockham.

River Thames

The mighty Thames forms the northern boundary of Surrey from the border with Berkshire at Runnymede in the west to the border with London at Thames Ditton in the east. For much of its history, Surrey extended further east along the south bank of the Thames to Rotherhithe, east of the City of London. The steady growth of London has meant that much of north-eastern Surrey has now been swallowed by Greater London.

The name of the Thames was recorded by the first Romans to arrive in Britain as 'Tamesis'. This word does not seem to have been used by the local Celtic peoples for anything other than the great river, but it may be linked to the word 'temeslos' that scientists think may have existed in even older Indo-European languages and which meant 'black' or 'dark'. If so, the Thames would mean 'The Dark River'. Others are unconvinced by this theory. They think that the Celts merely took over the name from the non-Indo-European peoples who inhabited Britain before the Celts came in, much the same way as the Romans took the name from the Celts and the English from the Romans. If this were the case then the name comes from a totally lost language and its meaning is unknown.

The River Thames in Surrey is the responsibility of the Environment Agency, which checks water quality, flooding problems and wildlife habitats. All boats on the Thames have to be registered with the agency and an annual fee paid to use the river. There is a speed limit of 4.3 knots on the Surrey section of the river – a rather clumsy figure that has resulted from the agency's insistence on using the metric system and imposing a limit of 8km/h.

River Tillingbourne

The Tillingbourne rises on the northern slopes of Leith Hill and runs westward along the south side of the North Downs. It flows through Friday Street, Abinger Hammer, Gomshall, Shere, Albury, Chilworth and Shalford before flowing into the Wey. From the sixteenth to the nineteenth century, the river provided power to a number of industrial mills making gunpowder and paper, as well as more conventional mills grinding flour. The clear waters of the stream made it ideal for the growing of watercress, which is still carried on here, and for fishing.

Welland Gill

This stream is one of the small streams that come together near Horley to form the River Mole. It rises in a pond, fed by a number of springs, near Upper Prestwood and flows north through Glover's Wood before veering east to pass south of Charlwood and join the Mole.

River Wey

The River Wey has two main branches, the Wey North and the Wey South, that meet at Tilford. The Wey South rises on Black Down, south of Haslemere. It then flows north almost to Haslemere before turning west to flow through Liphook, turning north-west to Bramshot and Bordon, then north-east to Lindford and Frensham to reach Tilford. A major tributary of the Wey South is the River Slea, which rises west of Kingsley and flows east, picking up the Oakhanger Stream before entering the Wey South near Headley Park. The Wey North rises near Alton in Hampshire and flows east to enter Surrey near Farnham. It then turns south to join with the Wey South.

The combined Wey heads east from Tilford to pass through Elstead, Godalming and Shalford to Guildford. After Guildford it heads to Pyrford, Byfleet and Addlestone to flow into the Thames at Weybridge.

In recent years there have been determined efforts to improve the quality of the water in the Wey. The numerous angling clubs located along the river are now able to go after chub, barbel, roach, pike, bream, carp, perch and even eels.

SWAN UPPING

In the third week of July each year the Thames in Surrey witnesses the ancient ceremony of Swan Upping. Three skiffs take part; one crewed by men appointed by the monarch, one by the Dyers' Company and one by the Vintners' Company – these last two being Livery Companies of the City of London. The skiffs head slowly upstream over the course of several days, each crew seeking to capture swans as they go. The Dyers mark their swans with a single leg ring, while the Vintners mark theirs with a ring on each leg and the royal swans are left unringed. In former times the birds were marked by having their bills nicked with a sharp knife, but such a practice is deemed unnecessary these days. The ceremony has been going on since the fifteenth century; before that time all swans on the Thames were deemed to belong to the monarch. Swans on other rivers generally belonged to the landowner through whose land the river flowed, though it was possible to rent out the right to take swans – or other waterfowl or fish – from the landowner. In 2009 Queen Elizabeth attended the Swan Upping for the first time, prompting a vigorous search of the records which revealed that no monarch had attended the ceremony for over 350 years.

EATING THE SWANS

These days only wild swans are found on the Thames, but in years gone by large flocks of tame birds were kept. The Windsor Flock was usually the largest, and in the year 1500 was recorded to be 2,000-strong. The birds were, of course, being raised for the table. Swans were usually eaten only by the rich since they were costly to raise properly. Three weeks before they were eaten, the birds had their wings clipped and were then kept away from the river in pens where they were fed exclusively on corn. This cleansed their flesh of the strong fishy flavour that it would have if the bird were slaughtered straight from the river. Once slaughtered, swans were hung for anything up to two weeks before being sent to the kitchens. As a rule, swans were eaten in the winter when fresh beef, lamb and pork were not available, Halloween to Lent being the traditional season.

A cook book from about 1480 gives instructions for cooking a swan. The bird is to be stuffed with pears, quinces, grapes, garlic and herbs, then roasted on the spit. When it is done, the stuffing is to be removed and mixed with red wine, cumin and the bird's blood, then the mixture is to be quickly boiled before being poured over the bird as it is presented at table.

RIVER POLICE

The Surrey Police have responsibly for safety and law enforcement on the River Thames between Runnymede and Teddington Lock. In 2006 Surrey Police gained a new river boat to help with their duties. It was launched at the Thames Motor Yacht Club at Hampton Court on 5 January by North Surrey's Divisional Commander Chief Superintendent Richard Morris. The boat was put into the care of Shepperton's PC Halstead, though it was expected that he would sometimes hand the boat over to staff from the Environment Agency when they needed to be out on this stretch of water. Previously the Thames in Surrey was the responsibility of the River Police section of London's Metropolitan Police. This was a hangover from medieval days when the Thames had been tidal to Thames Ditton, the construction of Teddington Lock meant that the tidal stretch ended there. The City of London had always been responsible for the tidal stretch of the river.

LOCKS IN SURREY

Locks are essential on rivers used by barges and other boats. They hold back water to keep the river above them deep enough for boats to use them, but allow those boats through to the lower level without letting the water flood out. Locks are also used on canals to move boats from one level to the next. The locks in Surrey stand on two waterways: the River Thames and the Wey Navigation Canal. The locks on the Thames were all rebuilt to their current design between 1812 and 1815. The locks on the Wey Navigation Canal date to between 1635 and 1671.

Thames Locks
Chertsey Lock
Shepperton Lock
Sunbury Lock
Molesey Lock

Wey Navigation Canal Locks
Thames Lock
Weybridge Town Lock
Coxes Lock
New Haw Lock
Pyrford Lock
Newark Lock
Papercourt Lock
Triggs Lock
Bowyers Lock
Stoke Lock
Millmead Lock
St Catherines Shalford Lock
Unstead Lock
Catteshall Lock

CROSSINGS OF THE THAMES

For centuries the City of London was responsible for the tidal Thames – which then reached deep into Surrey. It rigorously enforced a ban on any new bridges in order to force travellers to use London Bridge and so to use shops, taverns and inns in London rather than anywhere else.

The first bridge above London Bridge was Kingston Bridge which was erected where a bank of gravel made for firm foundations for the bridge piers. The first Kingston Bridge existed by about 900 and possibly much earlier. This bridge was of wood and had to be replaced at regular intervals. The bridge standing at Kingston in 1710 had twenty-two wooden piers – with two gaps in the centre wide enough for barges to navigate – and stood just downstream of the current bridge. In 1828 Kingston Town Council replaced the crumbling wooden bridge as it had many times before, but this time they used Portland stone and only four piers were needed. That bridge is still standing, though it has been widened several times.

Above Kingston Bridge stands Hampton Court Bridge. The first bridge here was erected in 1752 by a local man named James Clark, who believed that he could make a tidy profit on the construction cost by charging a toll. He was correct and in 1778 Clarke's first flimsy wooden structure was replaced with a more solid timber bridge. The construction of Molesey Lock by the City of London just upstream of the bridge changed the river flow, undercutting the piers and making the bridge dangerous. The then owner persuaded the City to pay him damages, so a new iron bridge was erected in 1864. In 1926 it was decided to link the Portsmouth Road to Hampton Court Bridge by constructing an entirely new, wide, straight road across the farmland between the two. The expected increase of traffic over the bridge led to the construction of a fourth bridge by the government that would be toll-free. The two-pier concrete and brick structure was opened in 1930 by the Prince of Wales.

Upstream of Hampton Court Bridge and Molesey Lock a passenger ferry runs from Hampton church to the south bank. It operates from March to October only.

At Walton-on-Thames there was a crossing by a ford that local historians think may have been used by Julius Caesar during his raid into Britain in 54BC (in 55BC he had not got further than Kent). By 1250 at the latest the ford had gone and was replaced by a ferry. In 1747 the local landowner replaced the ferry with a timber bridge on which he charged tolls. The bridge was famous for its complex design that not only allowed the central span to be 100ft wide but also allowed any timber to be removed for replacement without affecting the strength of the bridge so that it could remain open even when being repaired. In 1753 the famous bridge was painted by the great landscape artist Giovanni Antonio Canaletto. In 1788 it was replaced with a stone and brick bridge able to carry the traffic. That bridge suddenly collapsed during a storm in 1859 and was replaced by a steel structure that was made toll-free in 1870. In 1940 a German bomber narrowly missed the bridge, but the explosion did damage the foundations so a weight restriction was imposed that was never lifted. The bridge was demolished in 1985 by which time motor traffic was using a temporary fourth bridge built alongside. That temporary bridge was replaced in 1999 by another temporary structure while plans for a permanent replacement (under discussion since 1940) continued.

A second passenger ferry crosses the Thames at Shepperton, linking Ferry Lane on the north bank to Walton Lane on the south. The ferry runs year round from 10 a.m. to 5.30 p.m. It is first recorded in 1496, but may have been running for some time before then.

The bridge over the Thames at Chertsey as it appeared in the late nineteenth century.

A third ferry operated by Chertsey Abbey used to work just east of Chertsey. In about 1350 it was replaced by a timber bridge that the abbey kept in good repair and on which it charged tolls. When the abbey was closed during the Reformation the bridge was taken over by the Crown. The wooden structure was retained until 1784 when the current stone bridge was erected.

In 1971 an entirely new bridge was built over the Thames 500 yards upstream of Chertsey Bridge. It was constructed of concrete to carry the M3 and, like everything to do with motorways, is probably best described as 'functional'.

Almost as ugly is the iron and steel Staines Railway Bridge that was built by the London & South Western Railway Company in 1856. An effort was made to shape the six upright supports to resemble Greek Doric pillars, but this is marred by the current drab grey paint scheme.

The road bridge at Staines is much more elegant, having been built of white granite over three arches in the 1820s by architect George Rennie. In about AD 100 the Romans built a bridge at Staines upstream of the present bridge and used Church Island as a midway break. How long the Roman structure survived is unknown, but in 1228 documents show that a wooden structure stood on the same spot. It was regularly repaired until 1643 when it was destroyed during the Civil War. A hurriedly constructed timber replacement was then put up on the site of the present bridge and remained in use until 1791 when it was rebuilt in stone. That bridge was poorly constructed on weak foundations and the main arch cracked in 1799, so an iron replacement was put up that provided service until the current bridge was erected.

In 1930 the increasing traffic over Staines Bridge led to the construction of a bypass, now the A30. The bridge was designed by the eminent architect Sir Edwin Lutyens as a graceful brick and stone construction. It is still there, but is now rather overshadowed by the much larger 1984 concrete bridge that carries the M25 over the Thames. The motorway bridge was, for once, built with some care for its surroundings; the arches follow the same span and shape as the Lutyens bridge.

TRIBUTARIES OF THE WEY

River Slea	Lavant Stream
The Deadwater	Caker Stream
The Hollywater	West Brook
The Hanger	River Ock
Kingsley Stream	Warren Stream (from Warren Pond)
Oxney Stream	Tillingbourne
Frensham Stream	Stanford Brook
Northbrook	The Bourne

TRIBUTARIES OF THE RIVER MOLE

Dead River
Bookham Brook
Pachesham Brook
The Rye
Fetcham Mill Stream
Pipp Brook
Tanner's Brook
Shag Brook
Gad Brook
Wallace Brook
Leigh Brook
Baldhorns Brook

Deanoak Brook
Earlswood Brook
Salfords Stream
Burstow Stream
Spencer's Gill
Hookwood Common Stream
Gatwick Stream
Mans Brook (in Sussex)
Crawter's Brook (in Sussex)
Ifield Brook (in Sussex)
Reubens Gill (in Sussex)

MILLS ON THE MOLE

Horley Mill – demolished 1959
Sidlow – demolished 1790
Brockham – date of demolition unknown
Slyfield – date of demolition unknown
Downside – still standing, but not used as a mill
Cobham Old Mill – demolished 1953
Cobham New Mill – still standing in working order
Esher – demolished 1978
East Molesey Upper Mill – demolished 1780
East Molesey Lower Mill – still standing
Betchworth – although classed as 'hydro-electric turbines' the installations at Betchworth put in place in 2004 use water power as did the old mills. There are two 27.5kW turbines which feed electricity into the national grid.

11

SURREY AT WAR

RAF BASES IN SURREY DURING THE SECOND WORLD WAR

Dunsfold airfield began on 11 May 1942 when the Royal Canadian Air Force was given land near the village on which to build a fighter base. The base went operational on 16 October, a speed of construction that amazed the RAF. In 1946 Dunsfold was handed over to the RAF, which in turn handed it over to the Hawker Aircraft Company in 1951. Today its official role is as an emergency landing strip for Gatwick airport. More famously, however, it's the place where the BBC television show *Top Gear* is filmed.

Redhill airfield was built in 1934 to serve as the home base of the Redhill Flying Club, a private club catering to the well-heeled young men of Surrey who took up flying as a hobby. It was commandeered by the RAF when war broke out and became a pilot training base. In October 1940 it was converted into a night-fighter base. It was not until 1941 that the RAF got around to building barracks or other purpose-built structures, as until then the servicemen had made do by camping out in the club HQ. In 1943 day-fighters moved in, flying missions escorting bombers to attack targets in France and the Low Countries. In 1947 the airfield was returned to Redhill Flying Club, but that organisation renamed itself the Surrey and Kent Flying Club and moved to Biggin Hill in 1959. Redhill was taken over by Bristow Helicopters, which is still based at Redhill though they share the airfield with a glider club and other organisations.

Croydon airport was the main airfield serving London throughout the 1920s and '30s. It was here that Prime Minister Neville Chamberlain returned to Britain in 1938 to announce 'peace for our time'. When war broke out in 1939 Croydon was taken over by the RAF to serve as a major fighter base. It remained in RAF hands until 1946 when it returned to civilian use. However, the site was surrounded by houses and it proved impossible to extend the runway to handle the new breed of jetliners entering service in the 1950s. It closed in 1959. An impressively huge RAF monument stands beside the Purley Way.

RAF Kenley was established in 1917 by the Royal Flying Corps as a base for fighters protecting London. It remained in that role during peacetime and in 1937 underwent a modernisation programme that made it one the largest and most important fighter bases in southern England. It performed a key role during the Battle of Britain in 1940 and remained active throughout the war. In 1949 it became a training base for the Royal Auxiliary Air Force and was closed in 1974. The runways and many of the buildings still remain, having been put to good use by a gliding club and a number of businesses. A small monument stands beside Hayes Lane on the western edge of the old airfield.

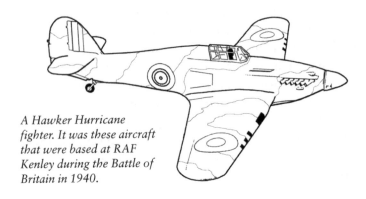

A Hawker Hurricane fighter. It was these aircraft that were based at RAF Kenley during the Battle of Britain in 1940.

Fairoaks airfield just outside Woking was a private airfield taken over in 1937 to serve as a pilot training centre. In 1940 it was converted to be a repair airfield to which lightly damaged aircraft would be flown to be properly repaired and tested before return to their squadrons. In 1946 Fairoaks was returned to its original owners. It remains a busy private airfield for light aircraft and helicopters.

In the 1930s Brooklands just outside Weybridge was home to Vickers Aircraft Ltd, which produced the Wellington bomber among other RAF aircraft. The adjacent airfield was used to fly off the completed Vickers aircraft, but was also a private airfield. The RAF took over when war was declared, though Vickers remained on site. The most famous product of the works was the bouncing bomb used to destroy the Ruhr Dams in 1943, designed here by Vickers' chief designer Barnes Wallis. Vickers remained at Brooklands until 1987, by which time they were part of British Aerospace. The airfield was then redeveloped for housing. The Brooklands Museum contains one of only two Wellington bombers to survive to the present day.

RAF Horne was located off Bones Lane, east of Smallfield. It opened in March 1944 to house three fighter squadrons on a temporary basis in the build-up to D-Day, which took place on 6 June that year. As soon as the Allied armies were established ashore, the squadrons flew out to an advanced base in France itself. Thereafter the base was used as an emergency landing field for damaged aircraft unable to make it home. In 1945 it was returned to farm use. A small plaque on the site carries the crests of the three squadrons based here for seven weeks in 1944.

RAF Cobham occupied the polo club playing grounds at Stoke D'Abernon. In 1940 it was used by Lysander observation aircraft based in Hampshire as a refuelling stop when on patrols in the eastern Channel. The RAF returned in 1944 when No. 652 Squadron was based here. This squadron was another observation unit flying Austers on reconnaissance missions over France as D-Day approached. They left on 25 July and the playing fields were returned to the polo club in 1945.

Wisley airfield was laid out in 1943 as a temporary base for the Vickers Aircraft Company based at nearby Brooklands. Many aircraft were repaired or serviced here during the war and in 1952 a permanent runway and hangars were erected. The site remained in use until 1973 when revised air control patterns centred on the expanding Heathrow made the site no longer viable for use as the sky above became to busy.

GIANT BALLOONS IN SURREY

During the Second World War a key defence against German bombers were the barrage balloons. These enormous silken monsters were filled with gas and tethered to the ground by a long steel cable. Each balloon was 62ft long and 25ft across. The steel cable was accompanied by a number of other cables dangling down from the balloon, each of which was stout enough to slice the wing off any aircraft foolish enough to fly underneath. The aim was not so much to down aircraft, as to force them to fly higher so that their bomb-aiming would be less accurate.

In Surrey, there was No. 2 Balloon Centre at Brooklands and No. 24 Balloon Centre at Redhill. Between them they controlled 135 balloons which floated above potential targets in Surrey itself or formed a defensive screen south of London.

BATTLES THAT TOOK PLACE IN SURREY

The Battle of Worplesdon (or Wimbledon), 568

The *Anglo-Saxon Chronicle* records Ceawlin and Cutha fought with Ethelbert and put him in to flight into Kent, killing two ealdormen at Wibbandune named Oslaf and Cnebba.

In 568 the richest and most powerful king in England was King Ethelbert of Kent, who derived much of his prestige from being the acknowledged English ally of the powerful Frankish kings on the continent. By contrast King Ceawlin of Wessex was something of a minor figure. With his son Cutha, however, Ceawlin was rapidly expanding Wessex power and prestige, largely at the expense of the post-Roman British in the west. The reasons for war between Kent and Wessex are not given, but since the main battle of the campaign took place in Surrey it is reasonable to assume that the two kingdoms were competing for control of Surrey and, perhaps, of the great merchant centre of London. At this date an ealdorman, from which our word alderman comes, was a nobleman holding power over some particular lands or function directly from the king.

An English warrior of the type who would have fought at Worplesdon. He has no armour, relying on his shield for defence. His main offensive weapon is the spear, with the sword being used for close combat. The men would have formed up shoulder to shoulder with their interlocked shields forming a 'shield wall' facing the enemy.

The unfortunate Oslaf and Cnebba would have been very senior Kentish government officials and nobles.

The victory seems to have fixed the eastern border of Wessex securely, for in 571 Ceawlin turned north to capture Aylesbury and Eynsham from the British and in 577 he took Bath, Gloucester and Dyrham as well.

The location of the battle has never been fixed with certainty. The place name Wibbandune is not recorded elsewhere, and may have been the original form of either Wimbledon or Worplesdon. Both sites have their supporters among historians, but the truth is that unless there is some lucky archaeological find we are unlikely to know exactly where the battle took place.

The Battle of Ockley, 851

The *Anglo-Saxon Chronicle* records, 'The heathen men then went south over the Thames into Surrey. And King Athelwulf and his son Athelbald with the West Saxon soldiers fought them at Ockley. There was made the greatest carnage of a heathen army that we ever heard of and they took the victory.'

The heathen men referred to are better known today as Vikings. This particular force had already captured Canterbury, defeated King Brihtwulf of Mercia somewhere near London (the site is not certain) and looted extensively up the Thames valley. The defeat of this force was a major early victory for the English.

A Viking warrior of the type who would have fought at Ockley. At this date the Vikings fighting in England were professional and highly trained warriors. He has a helmet and mail shirt, which indicates that he is a man of some importance, and wields the fearsome battleaxe.

The actual site of the battle is not entirely clear. The Vikings were clearly marching south along the old Roman road of Stane Street, now the A29 at this point. The West Saxons, often termed Wessex forces, were marching north from Chichester to confront the invaders. Tradition has it that the battle took place on the village green, an area of flat ground astride the road. However, Bucking Hill rises to over 100ft just north of the village. It would have made more sense for the Vikings to have deployed here where they would have the advantage of height over the advancing English. Perhaps some future archaeological dig might turn up some evidence for us.

The Battle of Farnham, 893

The *Anglo-Saxon Chronicle* records, 'Then Haestan and his force came in eighty ships and made camp at Milton. The force did not come out in full of this camp. They raided north of the Thames and took much plunder. Then Lord Edward rode with his army and fought them at Farnham, put the force to flight and seized the plunder. The Danes fled over the Thames and up the Colne to seek refuge on an island.'

Again this was a battle fought between the warriors of Wessex and the Vikings. The King of Wessex at this date was Alfred the Great, but he was in Devon facing a much larger Viking army encamped at Appledore. The Lord Edward fighting at Farnham was his eldest son, and later to be the king known as Edward the Elder who ruled from 899 to 924. Haestan was a noted Viking warrior and leader, though he does not seem to have been of noble or royal blood. The island in the Colne to which the Vikings fled is usually identified as Thorney, near Iver in Buckinghamshire. The Vikings were not strong enough to break out, but neither was Edward able to break in. After some weeks of watching each other, the two sides made an agreement under which the Vikings left Wessex leaving everything behind them, while Edward agreed to let them go. The fighting would go on for decades to come.

The Siege of Farnham Castle, 1216

In 1216 King John went back on all the promises he had made when agreeing to the Magna Carta the previous year. The nobles and Church rose in rebellion and a civil war ensued. Prince Louis of France came over to England posing as the champion of the old freedoms of the English and promising to implement the Magna Carta in full if he became king. Farnham Castle was held by men loyal to King John, and it was attacked by Louis in April as he sought to isolate London from the rest of the kingdom. The siege was over quickly as John's men knew that their lord was far away in Lincolnshire and that they could expect little help. Louis installed a garrison that held it for ten months. By then, however, John was dead and the new king was the boy Henry III whose regent, William Marshal, quickly solved the kingdom's problems and ended the civil war. Louis went back to France, evacuating Farnham as he went.

The Siege of Bletchingley Castle, 1264

In 1264, England was in turmoil. King Henry III had proved himself to be an inept and spendthrift monarch, though not an overly bad one, causing much unrest among nobles, merchants and peasants. A faction among the nobles led by Simon de Montfort, Earl of Leicester, was demanding that the nobles and leading commoners should at least be consulted by the king over taxation and spending decisions. Henry refused and both sides began mustering forces. Among the most powerful of the nobles opposing Henry was Gilbert de Clare, Earl of Hereford, who was nicknamed Red Gilbert because of his red hair. Gilbert owned lands in Surrey, most notably the castle at Bletchingley. Henry sent a force to capture the castle. After a short siege and with no prospect of help in sight, Gilbert's constable surrendered the fortress. The main strongpoint, a central square tower of stone, was pulled down but the earthworks left intact, and some of these remain to this day.

The Battle of Guildford, 1497

In 1497 yet another Scottish raid over the border prompted King
Henry VII to decide on a major retaliatory attack to punish the
Scots and teach them not to mess with the English. Traditionally
such attacks were made by forces raised in northern England
and financed by a tax levied in the northern shires – a similar
arrangement in the southern counties financed raids and attacks
against France. However, Henry opted to view the affair as
a major war and levied a tax on all England. This did not go
down at all well in the southern shires, with riots and protests
as a result. In the West Country and Cornwall in particular,
things were more serious and by May the Baron Audley was
leading an army of 15,000 armed men out of Somerset towards
London. Audley and his men arrived in Guildford early in June.
They found the royal army encamped at Hounslow, so Audley
pitched camp on the downs east of the town while sending out
messengers urging men from the south-eastern shires to rally to
the rebellion. On 14 June a force of 500 royal hobillars – men
equipped as infantry but given horses to carry them on raids –
appeared at Albury Down and attacked the outlying sentries set
by Audley. The rebels rushed to arms and a fight ensued over
what is now Pewley Down. After some sharp fighting, the royal
soldiers withdrew. The rebels marched on towards London, but
were defeated in battle at Deptford on 17 June. King Henry
chose to execute only two of the rebels, but he imposed savage
fines on the rest which not only boosted his royal coffers but
impoverished Cornwall for a generation.

The Siege of Farnham Castle, 1642

When the English Civil War broke out, the resident garrison
of Farnham Castle declared for Parliament. The commander,
George Wither, hurriedly began updating the defences which
had seen no major work since the 1490s. He had not got very
far when a Royalist army under Sir John Denham arrived.

Wither and his men fled. Denham then moved in and continued the work where Wither had left off. By December 1642, when a new Parliamentarian force arrived, the defences were much stronger, though by no means fully modernised. A desultory siege began, but when Sir William Waller arrived with modern siege artillery, Denham knew that he could not hold out. Rather than suffer a bloody assault, Denham negotiated a peaceful end to the siege and marched out with honour. Waller had neither the men nor the desire to garrison the castle, so he blasted a hole in its walls to make it useless as a fortress, then left.

The Attack on Reigate Castle, 1648

In the spring of 1648 a new civil war broke out in England as the harsh rule of Parliament after the defeat of King Charles I took hold. The rebellion began in Kent in May, prompting Henry Rich, Earl of Holland, to make a speech in Surrey supporting the uprising. By early July some 600 men had come armed to support Holland, among them George Villiers, Duke of Buckingham, and his younger brother Francis. Holland led his small force to attack Reigate Castle, then a store of weapons for the local militia garrisoned by a small Parliamentarian force. When the Royalists arrived they fired a few shots, after which the Roundheads fled north to Kingston. The two Villiers brothers led the few cavalry in the Royalist force in pursuit. They had just crossed Surbiton Hill and were riding down what is now Villiers Road when they were ambushed by men from the Kingston garrison. Francis was killed outright, and George unhorsed. Backing up against a tree, George Villiers drew his sword and managed to hold off a determined assault by no less than six Roundhead troops long enough for a comrade to bring him a horse on which he made his escape. Having looted Reigate Castle of anything useful, Holland led his men out of Surrey to join Royalist forces elsewhere.

AND ONE THAT DIDN'T:
THE BATTLE OF REIGATE

A hugely influential book was published in 1887 entitled *The Battle of Reigate*. It envisaged Britain being invaded by a hostile army from the Continent and followed the course of the fighting which culminated in a great battle fought at Reigate as the invaders sought to find a route over the North Downs to attack London. The book included not only the very latest military technology and tactics, but was the result of collaboration by several leading military figures. The conclusion of the book was that London was virtually defenceless – a similar conclusion to that reached by military planners in 1940 – and that any invader would need to be stopped at the Channel or met by sustained and dogged defence north of the capital. As a result the government established a chain of forts along the North Downs that were dubbed the 'London Defence Positions'.

The London Defence Positions
In 1889, largely as a result of *The Battle of Reigate*, the government ordered the construction of a chain of forts along the North Downs. These were constructed at:

Pewley Hill	East Merstham
Henley Grove	Fosterdown
Denbies	Woldingham
Box Hill	Betsoms Hill
Betchworth	Halstead (Kent)
Reigate	Farningham (Kent)

Each fort was intended to serve as a mustering place for the local militia and as an ammunition store for the professional army. They consisted of several reinforced magazines, plus living accommodation and a parade ground. Each was surrounded by concrete and earthwork defences that were to guard the fort against a surprise attack. The main battles, it was envisaged, would be fought across the hills and fields. In the event, Britain was not invaded. The forts continued to be used as mustering centres and ammunition stores for some years, most recently by the Home Guard during the Second World War.

The fort at Henley Grove is still in use as an educational centre, and is open to the public from time to time. The fort on Reigate Hill is owned by the National Trust and is open most days of the year. The others are either on private land or have been demolished.

MAJOR AIR RAIDS ON SURREY

Guildford, 13 October 1915

The first ever air raid on Surrey took place on the night of 13 October 1915 when a giant Zeppelin airship flew over the North Sea from Germany with orders to locate and bomb the explosives factory at the Albury Mill. The British had camouflaged the nearby St Martha's Church thinking that it made too obvious a landmark. The German captain spotted St Catherine's Church, mistook it for St Martha's and began bombing what he took to be Albury Mill beside the Tillingbourne. He was in fact hitting some industrial buildings beside the Wey. Nobody was killed in the raid, though several buildings were badly damaged. One swan, however, did pay the ultimate price.

Croydon, 15 August 1940

At 6.50 p.m. a force of twenty German bombers launched an attack on the RAF fighter base at Croydon. The bombers had come in low and evaded detection so that no air raid warning had been given. Fortuitously, fighters of No. 111 Squadron were returning to Croydon at the time and attacked the

Germans. This caused the attack to break up, so bombs fell over a wide area. One bomb hit the factory belonging to NSF just as the board of directors was meeting. Every single director of the company was killed instantly. The Bourjois Soap Factory was also hit, killing three workmen and halting production for the duration. In all, 62 people were killed and 137 injured, of whom 37 were kept in hospital for at least one night.

Kenley, 18 August 1940

At 1.20 p.m. the RAF base was hit by two German bomber forces coming in from different directions and at different heights. The Germans were attacked over Kenley by No. 615 and No. 32 Squadrons of Hurricanes that had flown in from Biggin Hill. They were in turn met by a heavy escort of Messerschmitt Bf109 fighters which pounced down from high above the German bombers. In all, seventeen RAF fighters were shot down and eighteen badly damaged, while the Germans lost twenty-one and fifteen damaged. On the ground, the base at Kenley lost three hangars (totally destroyed) and all buildings were damaged to some extent. Ten fighters were destroyed on the ground, and twenty-three more damaged.

Brooklands, 4 September 1940

At 1.20 p.m. six Junkers Ju88 bombers launched a low-level attack on the Vickers Aircraft factory at Brooklands accompanied by six Messerschmitt Bf110 fighters carrying bombs and escorted by a dozen Messerschmitt Bf109 fighters. The force had come in low and fast, evading both detection and defences. One 500kg bomb landed on the works canteen, where many workers were having lunch, and twenty-three other bombs hit the factory with other buildings nearby also being hit. In all, 75 men and 5 women were killed, 176 people required hospital treatment lasting at least one night and another 243 required some hospital treatment. Four of the bodies were so badly damaged that they could not be identified and were buried together in Burvale cemetery.

Bramley, 16 December 1942

A lone Dornier Do17 bomber came in low and fast on a hit and run raid around 4 p.m. as the light was fading. It attacked a train packed with Christmas shoppers just as it was pulling out of Bramley & Wonersh station. The plane strafed the train with machine guns and dropped a bomb which exploded on the embankment, narrowly missing the train. Seven people were killed, including the driver and guard, another forty-seven people had to be taken to hospital and the train was badly damaged. There would undoubtedly have been many more deaths but for the fact that a Canadian army unit was based nearby. The soldiers came running to the scene and administered first aid using their battlefield dressings.

Abinger Hatch, 18 August 1944

On this day a doodlebug came tearing through the air, hit a tree and cartwheeled into the ancient Church of St James where it exploded. An official report summed up the damage to the church which dated back to 1086. The west wall of the nave, including the belfry and spire and the great tie beam on which they were supported, plus all the roof of the nave, were completely destroyed. So too was the south door and porch, a great part of the north wall including three Norman windows and the south wall up to a point beyond the porch. The blast stripped all the roofs of the building, and the lych-gate, of their traditional Horsham stone slabs except for parts of the north face of the north aisle. Fragments of glass from all the windows lay outside. The pub opposite was also damaged, having its windows blown in and much of its roof stripped off. The church was rebuilt after the war, but then twenty years to the day after the V1 hit, the spire was struck by lightning and burned down.